A
Strange

616.9 Leibowitch, Jacques
LEI

#4.95   A strange virus of
         unknown origin

DATE		
FEB 2 5 1987		
DEC 0 6 1993		
DEC 8 1994		
JAN 0 4 1996		
MAY 2 9 1996		

© THE BAKER & TAYLOR CO

Cover design by Donald E. Munson
Book design by Iris Bass

A Strange Virus of Unknown Origin

Dr. Jacques Leibowitch

Translated from the French by
Richard Howard

With an Introduction by
Dr. Robert C. Gallo

AVAILABLE
PRESS

BALLANTINE BOOKS ● NEW YORK

Once we can name each part of our body, that body disturbs us less.

Milan Kundera,
The Unbearable Lightness of Being

CONTENTS

Foreword by Robert C. Gallo, M.D.   xi
Introduction to the American Edition   xiii
Introduction   xv

Part One   The History of AIDS and its Virus

1. Mounting Perils   3
    The Lavender Peril   3
    The Lavender Plague   7

2. Research   10
    On Method and Principles   10
    The Agent and Its Victims   11
    The Logic of the Prosecution   14
    Pitfalls   16

3. On the Trail of the Virus   20
    AIDS Geography: a Disease of Exotic Countries   20
        Equatorial Africa   21
        Japan   26
        The Caribbean   27
    A Disease of the T4-Lymphocytes   28
    The Desert of the Lymphocyte System   29
    The Mysteries of Propagation   30
        Through the Blood   30
        Syringes and AIDS   32
        Mother and Child   32
        AIDS and Sexuality   34
        In the Tropics: Insects and Syringes   38

4. Typical Portrait: Research Procedures   42
    Feline AIDS   44

5. AIDS, Signed HTLV?   48
    Who Is HTLV?   48
    T-Lymphocytes, Targets of HTLV   49
    The HTLV Virus in the World   51
    Contamination by HTLV   57
      Sexual Propagation   57
      The HTLV Virus Is Transmitted from Mother to Child   58
      The HTLV Virus Is Transmitted by Means of Blood Cells   59
    The Alibis Collapse   60
      A Scattered HTLV for a Limited AIDS?   60
      Aids Now and HTLV Permanently?   61
    The African Strain   65
      History of the Fevers of Marburg, of Lassa, and of Ebola   66
    Geopolitics of AIDS   67
    Confrontations and Final Conclusions   69
      The Kenyan Virus and the Cuban Pigs:
        the CIA through AIDS   69
      The Pasteur Virus   70
      Why was the HTLV Hypothesis Best?   70

            Part Two   The AIDS-Effect

1. Haiti, Infamy and Prejudice   77
    The Stigma of the Risk Group   78
    The Impact   79

2. The Blood Puzzle   81
    Which Blood Products Are Involved?   81
    Anti-Hemophiliac Fractions   82
    How Are the Anti-Hemophiliac Fractions Prepared?   83
    What Is the Source of the Blood Used in the Production
      of Anti-Hemophiliac Fractions?   85
    To Identify Contaminated Blood   86
    The AIDS Virus Is Not Transmitted Like the
      Hepatitis B Virus, But Like HTLV-I   86
    Anxiety as to Certain Products   87

Contents

3. AIDS, Homosexuality, Doctors, Society   90
   A Modern Disease, or an Archaic Disease in a
      Modern World?   90
   AIDS and Medicine in Mutation   92
   AIDS à l'Américaine   93
   Medicine Disturbed   94
   Waiting for Biology   96

Part Three   AIDS: The Clinical Picture

1. Overall Description of the Disease: the Course of an Infection
      by HTLV-III/LAV   101

2. Early Symptoms of Infection by HTLV-III/LAV   107
   Nonspecific Symptoms   107
   Kaposi's Sarcoma   110
      Observation No. 1   111
      Observation No. 2   112
   Outcome of the HTLV-III/LAV Infection   112

3. Later Symptoms of the Infection by HTLV-III/LAV   114
   Secondary Infections   114
   Which Development?   116

4. Tests and Examinations Indicating an Infection from
      HTLV-III/LAV   117
   Direct Tests   118
   Indirect Tests   119
      Biopsy of a Kaposi's Sarcoma Lesion   119
      Biopsy of a Lymph Node   120
   Tests Evaluating the Degree of Immune Deficiency   121

5. Understanding the Symptoms of the Disease   129
   Fever, Fatigue, Weight Loss, Swollen Lymph Nodes   129
      Endopyrogenes   129
      Alpha Interferons   130
   Kaposi's Disease   131
      Is Kaposi's Sarcoma a Cancer?   131
      Is Kaposi's Sarcoma a Disease of Homosexuals?   132

Kaposi's Sarcoma and Cytomegalic Infections 133
New Hypotheses for Kaposi's Sarcoma 134
Secondary Infections from Opportunistic Germs 137
The T4-Lymphocytes, Predators of Intracellular Microbes? 137
Malignant Tumors Complicating AIDS 138
Unexplained Symptoms 139

6. Immunological Anomalies and Infections Observed in
    Homosexuals 140
    "Tropical" Intestinal Infections 140
    Superficial Lymph Node Swelling in Homosexuals 141
    Immunological Anomalies of Healthy Homosexuals 142
    Bruises and Black-and-Blue Marks, Hemorrhagic Tendency
    in Homosexuals 144

7. Treatments and Prospects 146
    Disseminated Kaposi's Sarcoma 146
    Should All Kaposi's Sarcoma Cases Be Treated? 147
    Secondary Infections 148
    Immune Deficiency 149

8. How Not to Catch HTLV-III/LAV 151
    Cells and Virus Carriers 151
    From the Viewpoint of the Virus Carrier 151
    The HTLV-Leukemia Model in Japan 151
    Is the Japanese Kiss Intransitive? 152
    Is Japanese Sexuality a Special Kind? 152
    The Route of Sperm and of Blood 153
    From the Viewpoint of the Receiver of the Contaminated
    Secretions 153
    Who Is a Virus Carrier? 153
    In the Absence of Symptoms, Can the Virus-Portage
    Be Detected? 154
    AIDS in Tropical Zones 154

Afterword 156

Acknowledgments 158

Bibliography 160

FOREWORD

THE WORD AIDS CAUSES FEAR IN SOME GROUPS, RAISED EYEBROWS and "off-color" jokes in others, but misconceptions in most. To many biomedical scientists and clinicians it meant a challenge to solve a mysterious, exotic, and fatal epidemic so linked to personal sexual habits, life styles and special medical and social problems that it was bound to provoke all segments of society. There has been nothing quite comparable to this problem in modern biomedical history. Just at a moment when prominent medical scientists were predicting the end of the great human infectious epidemics, AIDS entered the most technologically advanced societies in a manner stranger than science fiction. By a combination of interdisciplinary investigations, the cause of this disease was solved in 1984. AIDS is caused by a new virus called HTLV-III (human T-cell lymphotopic virus type III) or LAV (lymphadenopathy associated virus). The virus is of a type known as a retrovirus. The AIDS retrovirus is distantly related to two human retroviruses discovered earlier, known as HTLV-I and HTLV-II. Although we have learned a great deal about this virus family, they were only discovered at the end of the 1970's. They all infect the T-cell or T-lymphocytic, a cell which is of central importance to our immune system. Whereas HTLV-I and -II make the T-cell grow excessively, infection with the AIDS virus, HTLV-III, does the opposite. The infected T-cells die prematurely. HTLV-III is also rather closely related to retroviruses of ungulates (sheep, cattle, and goats); those viruses also cause chronic debilitating disease. For example, we now know the AIDS virus of man is closely related to a virus of sheep which causes a chronic neurological disease.

How did this disease begin? Where did the virus come from? How was it found? What is the evidence that it is the cause? What are the characteristics of the disease? The author, Jacques Leibowitch, describes the events leading to the discovery. He takes us through some of the reasoning processes that led to the virus as well as some of the misleading hypotheses. He draws our attention to the disease, its many pathological manifestations, its special social problems and stigmas. While emphasizing the human aspects Leibowitch constantly returns to the problem at the level of the cell and the special social problems of the patient and the carrier. He directs us to the concerns of the future: how to best use the new information.

Jacques Leibowitch is a clinical immunologist. He has been dedicated to the resolution of this disease since its inception. Located in Paris, he and his colleague Professor Saimot focused on the African cases seen in former French Africa. They were among the first to bring this lead on the origin of the virus to our attention. No one in the world has been closer to the problem in breadth of interest: the science, the patient, the cause, the care, the personal and social problems of the afflicted. Constantly speculating, constantly probing and provoking his colleagues, Leibowitch was highly instrumental in stimulating scientists to work just a bit harder to solve the AIDS riddle. This book bears witness to his passionate commitment and his willingness to plunge into the controversial issues. The reader will learn a great deal about the disease and its origin but will come away with the realization that a description of how we will effectively treat this disease, how we will prevent it, and how the virus kills the T-cell are all subjects for a future book.

Robert C. Gallo, M.D.
Chief, Laboratory of Tumor Cell Biology,
National Cancer Institute
November, 1984

INTRODUCTION TO THE AMERICAN EDITION

DISCOVERY OF THE AIDS VIRUS IS NOW OFFICIAL, ACCORDING TO simultaneous announcements in the United States and in France. Five years after the outbreak of the disease, both countries agree in designating as the culprit a certain type of virus, related to a microbe family whose first specimens had been discovered in the United States and in Japan around 1980.

If the "American" virus does not bear the same name as the "French" one, this discrepancy is merely a nomenclatural dispute, for there is no doubt that both countries have identified an extremely similar virus. And throughout the world, other research teams are now at work confirming what the inspired French and American investigators were first to discover: AIDS is the result of a viral infection; the virus in question is indeed an exotic one, probably from central Africa.

Is the announcement of this discovery premature? Granted, AIDS is far from vanquished; we must wait until truly lifesaving treatments are developed, until vaccines can be proposed, until we understand why and how some subjects are contaminated by the AIDS virus yet seem unaffected by it, while others die from it. But on one point AIDS is already defeated—a crucial point for those who have contracted or are threatened by it: The mysteries, the fantasies, with their pejorative or metaphysical resonances, have been dispelled for good. It is a serious disease, but henceforth AIDS is no more than one infectious disease among many others.

Primarily a history of this scourge, what follows is the first and dramatic part of an epic in which sufferers, doctors, and scientists—in their various ways—have inspired the research leading to demystification.

INTRODUCTION

NEW YORK UNIVERSITY HOSPITAL, 1979. DR. L., IN THE SECTION for the treatment of tumors and blood diseases, is perplexed: two young men in succession have consulted him about a skin disease extremely rare at their age, *Kaposi's sarcoma*. Neither patient has the Mediterranean family background almost always found in classic Kaposi's cases—Jewish forebears from central Europe, Armenian, Italian, or North African antecedents. True, both are homosexuals, but in New York, in 1979, there is no conclusion to be drawn from that.

During 1980, nothing much occurs to which these two first victims can be medically related. Nothing till 1981, when, in the course of several meetings of physicians working on the East Coast, it is learned that there are, in the area, a number of cases analogous to the first two. And these patients are also young homosexual men. The physicians realize that something abnormal is occurring in the medical realm, and they bring the matter to the attention of the National Centers for Disease Control in Atlanta, Georgia.

Atlanta, June 5, 1981. On Dr C.'s desk at the CDC, the ledger for the distribution of pentamidine to American hospitals: five patients, in the last month, have received the antibiotic used against a single microbe: pneumocystis carini. A strange name, but a common germ, occurring throughout the world, harmless in everyone except those whose immune shield is deficient. Five patients in one month is many more than normal; still more abnormal, these patients are young men in whom nothing can account for the serious pneumonias related to this microbe. These young men have no known reason for being in such a state of immune deficiency. They live in Los Angeles. They are homosexuals.

The history of AIDS (acquired immune deficiency syndrome) has officially begun. The "homosexual mystery" will dominate the beginning of the story: a notion that will shackle the minds of those too closely concerned with it.

January, 1982. Initially incredulous, administrators of the CDC must now deal with 202 victims—202 cases of an indubitably new disease, breaking out in the most hygienized regions of the Western world. And 96 percent of them are homosexuals. Certainly a matter for inquiry, if not for inquisition: *Time* and *Newsweek* magazines, as well as a sector of the medical community, light the first coals; they will soon be followed by most newspapers.

December 1981–January 1982. The fatal words have been uttered: "An epidemic is spreading like wildfire..." The *New England Journal of Medicine* and the London *Lancet,* weeklies read by nearly 100,000 physicians throughout the world, publish five articles signed by five different groups of authors. Five independent presentations with evident links: serious infections and/or Kaposi's sarcoma, these are the manifestations common to all these first victims.

February 1982. In Paris, a deputy of the rightist opposition puts a cunning question to the (then-Communist) minister of health: how to protect our young men against a plague of homosexuality said to be—like certain roses—"climbing." Granted, American physicians have already raised the semantic ante by inventing the label GRID (for "Gay-Related Immuno-Deficiency").

These first signs do not look good—for patients (the recorded death rate is a staggering 40 percent in a few months), for politicians, or for physicians. Immunology, the biomedical discipline that is directly concerned by this new "immunodeficiency," is one of the youngest fields of study. It has not yet had its baptism by fire. A group of physicians volunteer to try and participate in answering the main questions:

What is this new disease? Who is affected by it? What are its symptoms? How is it transmitted? What is its cause? Where does it come from—and why now? The first tactical objective of physicians the world over, all concerned by this explosion, will be to untangle the imbroglio—as fast as possible. To do so, a vast investigatory process of cross-checking research in the USA, the Caribbean, Europe, Japan, and also Africa, will be initiated. Concurrently the detective-physician is born, a hybrid of Dr. Livingstone and Inspector Colombo. His first (false) lead: the lavender peril.

·*Part One*·

THE HISTORY
OF AIDS
AND OF ITS VIRUS

· 1 ·

MOUNTING PERILS

The Lavender Peril

IN THE FIRST QUARTER OF 1982, THEN, THE HOMOSEXUAL STAMP IS affixed to the disease: Gay Related Immune Deficiency (GRID). The ambiguity of this designation involves or provokes a whole series of indiscreet interrogations as to the "mysteries of homosexual practices": an immunity disease linked to the homosexual condition. Thus wakened, suspicions will venture into hitherto restricted territory: the sweaty atmosphere of back-room bars, the swirling mists of bathhouses, the physical violence of certain contacts, and a record-holding promiscuity. When they come to write the history of AIDS, socio-ethnologists will have to decide whether the "practitioners" of homosexuality or its heterosexual "onlookers" have been the more spectacular in their extravagance. The homosexual "life style" is so blatantly on display to the general public, so closely scrutinized, that it is likely we never will have been informed with such technico-phantasmal complacency as to how "other people" live their lives.

It is a noisy and alarming debut, in the worst Hollywood manner, with the appropriate slogans ("homo-" this, "homo-" that). Successful as such campaigns rarely are, and as if to confuse the issue a little further, a stick of medical dynamite (GRID) with its long—far too long—fuse. Yet AIDS is not a disease specifically linked to the homosexual condition—and never has been. Viruses, even in 1984, cannot recognize their homosexual victims as such, and no one in biology has ever regarded such a thing as conceivable. On the other hand, in January 1982, there is no avoiding the possibility that some toxic product especially utilized by homosexuals might be at the origin of the epidemic.

The model of adulterated and toxic Spanish olive oil is there in everyone's mind. It will be recalled that in the previous summer of 1981, Spanish olive oil had a bad press because a fraction of the national product contained, for reasons still obscure, one or several toxins, with the most serious effects. Now, Homosexuals use "poppers" which are made of a chemical product with an extremely high rate of evaporation (and the smell of banana oil): amyl nitrite and its derivatives. The chemical was originally marketed in sealed glass ampoules which broke open with a loud pop. Some consumers are so enthusiastic that they have replaced the ampoule with a flask, and the clumsily administered soaked cotton held under the nose by a binasal forked straw thrust into its opening. In this fashion, gallons of poppers have been coursing through gay nostrils. Yet this product has been widely used for 30 years and not only by homosexuals. Therefore, in order to account for Gay-AIDS, it was necessary to invent the "contaminated popper" and its hypothetical marginal connections.

In this initial period, Parisian physicians are not inactive. During the first quarter of 1982, there are no more than five cases in the city, but there is every indication that this immunological disease will soon "gain" Europe, whatever its origins. Has there not been a tremendous expansion of transatlantic links, accompanying the dollar's fall in relation to the franc at the end of the 1970's, and consequently the rise of American cultural models? Had not France's own homosexuals imported the sobriquet *gai?* (Though the word's semantic wealth is scarcely equivalent, in French, to the English—originally, Old High German—source.*) Were not poppers of Ameri-

---

*For example, in venery, *gay* describes an animal that carries its tail high.

can manufacture—or label, at least—flooding the market in Amsterdam, only a few hours from Paris?

The first cases then seen in Paris permit the hypothesis that an "American pollutant consumed there" might be involved. The few Frenchmen infected have had, *in most cases,* New York contacts. Without being absolutely convinced of this hypothesis, but lacking a better conductor, we inform the CDC, with the diligent assistance of gay physicians, as to the brands of poppers used in Paris, their apparent origin, and their principal distributors. We also draw up a brief memorandum summarizing the facts and speculations concerning the disease, a study sent in February 1982 to our colleagues in the hospital services of Paris who, by reason of their specializations, would soon be seeing such cases in their wards. Simultaneously, a think tank is organized, working in voluntary cooperation with the Ministry of Health. Finally, since despite the absolute darkness in which everyone is working, it seems that matters have "begun" in North America, the milieu of the Franco-American jet-set must be informed: the American Hospital in Paris, the Palace (a nightclub famous at the time, frequented—among others—by globe-trotting gays), and Fréquence Gaie (the gay radio station). The message was: "Attention America—Stop—Danger. Stop Poppers, baths, back rooms, or other such festivities. Stop—Stop Everything." And no one indulged in too many illusions as to the impact of such a message!

The poppers fable will become a Grimm fairy tale when the first cases of AIDS-without-poppers are discovered among homosexuals absolutely repelled by the smell of the product and among heterosexuals unfamiliar with even the words *amyl nitrite* or *poppers*. But, as will be habitual in the history of AIDS, rumors will last longer than either common sense or the facts would warrant. The odor of AIDS-poppers will hover in the air a long time—long enough for dozens of mice in the Atlanta epidemiology labs to be kept in restricted cages on an obligatory sniffed diet of poppers 8 to 12 hours a day, for several months, until, nauseated but still healthy, without a trace of AIDS, the wretched rodents were released—provisionally—upon the announcement of a new hypothesis: *promiscuity.*

American homosexuals who have contracted AIDS are classified in two groups: those who have had fewer than 70 "partners" in the last year, and those who have had more. Half the cases are to be found among the "more than 70" cases. And certain virtuosos exceed 1,000, a numerical vertigo which would cause them difficulties in mere accounting. One of our French patients, in order to answer our indiscreet inquiries with some degree of accuracy, resorted to his pocket calculator before being able to announce his figure for the last year: 640. This homophiliac promiscuity is rich in metaphors, a source of much reflection and invention occasionally productive in biology. But the subject leads to certain ambiguities, and by a kind of sociobiological projection, the notion of "immune overexertion" is devised. As a matter of fact, highly promiscuous homosexuals often contract, in the course of intimate contacts, various infections (veneral diseases, hepatitis, herpes, cytomegalo-virus, amoebas, and several other "tropical pathologies"). An "immune overexertion"—a metaphorical echo of sexual overexertion—would result from such behavior. The immune system would have to confront these microbes as well as the medications prescribed against them. These could be especially *stimulating,* for the immune system which takes the "strange" in its stride, whether natural (microbic) or synthetic (medicinal). The riddle of Gay-AIDS could thus be solved in a simplistic concept. We all experience mental overexertion (so we commonly think); why not from excessive solicitations "immune fatigue" to the point of "exhaustion"? However, this hypothesis has two intrinsic weaknesses: first by too strongly titillating the immune system, as in the case of a muscle by its intensive utilization, one *swells* rather than flattens it. The functioning of the immune system which occurs as a consequence of stimulations, *creates* the organ and not the other way around; or so our professors have taught us, some of whom, however, are close to reversing themselves in the face of the AIDS "problem." Secondly, despite the statistical mayonnaise in which a taste for the strongest flavors prevails at the expense of the most discreet, there are at the time known cases of Gay-AIDS among decorously monogamous gentlemen. Even if the analysis by totalization tends to overlook their existence, there are at least several dozen (!) homosexuals with faithful partners or faithful to their partners, and in these couples AIDS is seen to strike not the fire-breathing dragon of the bars but the faithful homebody. Such monogamous cases should do away with the theory of the immune fabric crushed beneath a mountain of cataplasms or microbes! But nothing rational seems likely to halt the wave thus breaking, perhaps too long withheld in its gestation behind the dam of the new civil rights. And indeed, within months, it breaks up in a very unexpected original version. Sperm itself becomes the accursed agent of immune over exertion: Sodom and Gonococci are the latest duo acting the Gay-AIDS drama. Learned physicians and specialists announce the advent of a mutant immuno-suppressor "Ante/Sperm." Some devilishly transformed semen, and recently so too, for as we attempt to remind the prophets of that killer brand of sperm, Greeks long since, and other Mediterranean peoples, or some of them, sailors occasionally, and even women have been exposed for some thousands of years to the spermatic peril without turning it into a lymphocytic anemia. Nevertheless immuno-exhausting sperm is granted a certain credibility and money, enough for countless (but counted) mice to undergo the supreme indignity: human sperm injected . . . intravenously. Announcement of the first AIDS cases after blood transfusion in July–August 1982 will discredit without further (futile) polemics the Khomeinis of pestilential semen.

The Lavender Plague

During July and August 1982, the "multifactorial" house of cards hastily built around male homosexuality suddenly collapses: cases of AIDS are discovered in women, in hemophiliac children, in male heroin addicts, in a baby receiving transfusions at birth, and in a certified heterosexual receiving transfusions in Haiti. Henceforth AIDS is transmissible by transfused blood or its derivatives—a piece of information fraught with consequences, the first of which is that blood taken from a donor by puncturing a vein at his elbow does not carry spermatozoa! Blood contains cells (red corpuscles, white corpuscles, platelets) and plasma. If the "thing" carrying AIDS is found in the blood mixture, then the AIDS agent is most likely to be a microbe.

The homosexual community, increasingly hard hit by the growing number of cases, comes out of its isolation, or as some called it, ghetto (sometimes written GAY-TO): "they" are no longer the only victims, and the phrase "Gay Related Immuno-" should thereby die out. However, the switch from sperm to blood is not going to make sharing any easier. The transmission of the disease outside of "homosex" opens the prospect of a microbic apocalypse *tomorrow*. And the great panic begins.

Just for good measure, the Centers for Disease Control decides that AIDS offers a certain resemblance to hepatitis B. Hepatitis B and its virus are transmitted by blood and blood products, as well as during intimate contact. Hence AIDS "is transmitted like hepatitis B." The bomb is dropped.

The repercussions of this monumental analogical mushroom-cloud is enormous. Handlers of human blood, candidates for transfusion, industrial workers in blood products, then nurses and orderlies, garbage-men and embalmers, ambulance-drivers and first-aid workers, paramedics and prison guards, certain police officers, and even journalists working on AIDS stories, down to the toothbrush glass and finally any glass at all—everyone is panic-stricken and everyone speculates. The AIDS scourge, the lavender plague, and even the notion of a lavender star to indicate the pariahs, everything is suggested, argued, vituperated, until, little by little, facts and thoughts return. If AIDS is transmitted by the same means as hepatitis B, this sole analogy of *itinerary* affords no information as to the resemblance between AIDS and hepatitis B in general. Now, it will gradually appear that the contagiousness of AIDS has not so much in common with that of hepatitis B. No doctor, no employee in the paramedical sector, has contracted the disease through the habitual conditions of professional exercise, in which frequency of contamination from the virus of hepatitis B can be measured by up to 20 percent.

Along with this shatter comes a silver lining: AIDS (without Gay) rises to the top of the hit parade of American public health. Public enemy number one pulls down some 14 million additional dollars. The politicians raise the stakes even higher. Thirty million. Do I hear a better bid? Physicians and biologists are going to intervene in vast numbers. But to do what?

Medicine, geared with all its diplomas, at first flabbergasted, just cannot believe what it perceives. Like its impotent ancestors, Western medicine (and particularly American medicine, most strongly fortified with the discourse of science and technology) incredulously hears and scouts the rumble: the formidable infectious landslide of this century's turn is rolling near.

For medical biology, a war has just been declared. Medical speeches are filled with those imprecations which fustigate the foe and threaten it with harsh antibiotic or vaccinal reprisals. But to begin the campaign, the cartographers of the medical general staffs have no intelligence about the "alien" regimental rolls: AIDS is unknown. Yet this riot must be calmed, this wind of madness which sows panic and feeds on panic.

To disentangle, to decipher, to classify, to give a meaning to all this chaos, the first requirement is to understand what is happening. Medicine hastily must know, and reveal what it knows. Where, how, who, why, since when, and, as fast as possible, through whom does the evil come?

2

RESEARCH

AMONG ALL THE LINES OF INVESTIGATION TO FOLLOW, THERE IS one which must urgently be pursued: what is the agent of AIDS? An answer to this would permit putting the question in rational terms, the first indispensable step toward the knowledge that would lead to the conquest of AIDS.

On Method and Principles

To find the agent is not that simple. It will take skill and, no doubt, luck. But in order to minimize the aleatory imponderables, it will also take principles, what are called "epistemological" principles, capable of organizing *a priori* the procedures necessary to the progress of the research.

Among the thousand and one hypotheses which the facts might suggest, choose the "least costly." The scientific cost of a hypothesis can be estimated in terms of the number of uncertainties and speculations it introduces, or else in terms of time—*i.e.,* the time necessary for its verification by facts. Hence there is a choice to be made among a series of possible hypotheses. All hypotheses are not equally good. The best will be the one which, at the least scientific cost, will permit the likeliest connection of the maximum number of facts by which the disease is characterized. At the same time, the best hypothesis will have a high productivity: the procedures necessary for its verification should increase the knowledge of the disease and of its mechanisms.

The Agent and Its Victims

To find ... what? First suspects among any microbes: viruses. For a virus, in particular, can exhibit the long delays which separate contamination from the disease's appearance after a blood transfusion. No toxin could be present in the blood for so long without that individual's being distressed. Viruses, on the other hand, can be carried by apparently healthy individuals.

A virus is a microparticle measured in hundreds of nanometers, visible only to the electronic microscope. Viruses must be enlarged anywhere from ten thousand to a hundred thousand times in order to be photographed. The chemical constituents of a virus are diverse, but the portion essential to its survival is nucleic acid, which contains the information necessary to its functioning and reproduction. This structure is endowed with properties that permit it to be "copied," hence reproduced. But the viral nucleic acid is incapable of copying itself, and the virus must borrow the necessary ingredients from the cell: cellular printing, machinery, raw materials, and energy. Viruses are by definition intracellular parasites. Certain viruses, by multiplying within the host cell, can cause its death by explosion (lytic viruses). Others are more readily tolerated. They are "supported" by the host cell, which permits their reproduction without perishing from it.

A certain number of viruses can also be integrated within the chromosomes* of the host cell. The viral nucleic acid is lodged somewhere in one or several regions of the cellular nucleic acid into

---

*Chromosomes are, within the cell nucleus, the visible form of stockpiling the nucleic acids.

which it infiltrates. This genetic addition will have variable effects on the cell's functioning. Thus placed at the controls of the cellular machinery, the virus may, for instance, promote the release of an excessive amount of substances which the cell habitually produces in infinitesimal quantity. The consequences of this overproduction vary according to the nature of the constituent produced. If it be an enzyme capable of cutting through the intracellular armature, it will risk making the cell lose certain internal elements necessary to its maintenance within the ensemble of neighboring cells. ("Cancerous transformation" may be the spectacular result of an insertion of viruses into the nucleus of a cell. "Transformed," it multiplies without the brake normally provided by the physical contact of its neighbors.) The normal cells secrete "hormonal" substances intended for the neighboring cells. (A cell in a culture is like a snail on a lettuce leaf: it exudes.) "Transformed" because a virus has inserted itself within its nucleus, the cell may massively secrete these hormones without the modifications that lead to "cancerization" necessarily occurring. For AIDS, in which the investigation will designate a virus capable of inserting itself within the nucleus of the host cell, we shall be led to postulate this type of "transformation."

A virus integrated into the chromosome of the host cell can also remain latent without perceptibly modifying the behavior of the cell which harbors it. In this case, the virus's presence is detectable only in the form of a "surplus" of information corresponding to the sequence of the viral nucleic acid, a surplus in relation to the information contained in the nucleus of a virgin cell. Among viruses, the *retroviruses* represent a huge family. They are capable of "reversing the direction" of viral nucleic acid to cellular nucleic acid, possessing the chemical equipment which permits copying itself before "returning" into the chromosome. "REverse TRanscriptase" is the enzyme, the instrument of this "return," hence the prefix RETRo. By reason of this capacity, retroviruses are especially apt to induce phenomena of "transformation" within the cell they infect.

Where do viruses come from in the history of the world of living beings? The prevailing hypothesis is that they represent nucleic acid fragments from some mother cell on which they remain dependent; a virus would be an off-cut in the editing of a chromosome tape which broke off some million years ago in the course of Cell History; a tiny submarine, mobile within cellular space, detached from the mother chromosomic station to which it perpetually tends to return, lacking any real autonomy.

To find a virus specific to AIDS will first of all consist in recognizing and linking the facts concerning AIDS more or less closely, though detours will sometimes seem to be long ones. Through the symptoms of the disease and the organs affected, we shall recognize the cells which the virus might infect. This will be a major element of information: show us whom you frequent and we will be closer to finding out who you are. To collect a worldwide account of the disease and to draw its contour on a planisphere: tell us where you hang out. Try to retrace the AIDS route through the world and through the world's history—how AIDS "reached" the USA. Such historico-geographic reconstruction might give us characteristic clues. The virus's interhuman route (by which means it passes from one human to another) will afford us a further lead. Then to construct a robot-portrait of the culprit, which we shall then compare with those of already known disease-causing viruses. To circulate information and the state of research via medical "interpol" by all means possible: conferences, seminars, colloquia, publications, telephone calls. Starting from facts, bearing in mind the signaletic dossier of the agent-type, we must show that the suspect being sought is present in each of the patients.

How is the presence of the phantom virus in a given subject to be exposed? As a minimal life form, the virus can *reproduce,* with the help of the host cell from which it borrows all its vital supplies. The virus will reproduce all the better if the supportive cell does also. If we can identify which cell is likely to harbor the virus we seek, and have it multiply in the laboratory-greenhouses by providing the right *fertilizer* which that cell type requires, and if during cell multiplication the searched virus consents to reproduce as well, then we might have a chance to snap a picture of it under the lenses of an electronic microscope. But its photography will not suffice to identify it precisely; viruses producing very different effects can have the same ultramicroscopic silhouette. Hence it will be necessary to pursue it further by chemical means. What are its constituents—in sugar, in proteins, in nucleic acids? For this we must resort to the ultrasophisticated techniques of molecular biology.

With the help of tracer molecular probes,* we shall try to collect, within the chromosomic hieroglyphs, a segment of nucleic acid alien to the host cell which may be that of a virus.

Lacking these techniques, or conjointly with them, another method of identification—a much less arduous one—can ultimately be explored. Multiplying viruses have the fortunate impudence of exposing their molecules on the surface of the host cells. Not only do they distort, for the sole goal of reproduction, the essentials of the cellular machinery, but they also plant their own proteins on the surface of the victim cell—surfaces which the lymphocyte patrols are responsible for inspecting down to the tiniest molecular recess. The immune cells mark the posted sign "alien" and secrete the alert. Antibodies form, and if they do not suffice to free the organism from this viral piracy,† they indirectly signal the presence of a virus in an individual, as will be revealed by a simple blood sample.

The Logic of the Prosecution

To discover a virus at the scene of the disease will not prove its responsibility. We must still scrupulously verify its timetable in relation to the history of the patient and that of the disease. For a disease new to the Western world, the virus must have been newly

---

*Tracer molecular probes are *inverted* copies of the virus's sequence of nucleic acid. These countertypes have the property of pairing very powerfully with the nucleic acid of the virus of which they are the inverted copy. These probes are deliberately "marked" according to various procedures and hence discoverable. Therefore they can be "traced"—within a chromosome, for example.

†Because viruses are mainly *within* the cell they infect, hence inaccessible to the antibodies.

introduced into that part of the globe (North America, Europe). In a given patient, the virus must be there *beforehand* if we are to make it a plausible culprit, for if it was recognized only *after* the beginning of the disease, it would obviously be innocent, at best merely one of those numerous opportunist microbes profiting from the loss of immune defenses in order to colonize a few defenseless cells.* The formal indictment of the suspect will remain the most difficult part of the investigation, since in fact we undertake our research on a subject who is already ill. Unless we have blood samples from *before* the disease, which would permit, after the fact, reconstituting the following unambiguous sequence: in the blood of the still apparently healthy subject, the silent presence of the virus,† then the disease. Since 1976 the refrigerators of the CDC have kept sera of volunteers participating in a medical investigation since that date. Some among them have AIDS today. These are what medical jargon rather brutally calls "informative patients"—as well as exceptional ones.

But concurrently the investigations continue so as to accumulate elements of proof which converge on the suspect(s). The transition from suspect to culprit occurs gradually, in proportion to the quality of the links established between a given virus and the disease. We then attempt, in the laboratory, the reconstruction of the crime. Target cells from healthy subjects are exposed to the virus in order to verify that its behavior in a test tube, *in vitro,* mimics or reproduces at least certain of its effects in the patient, *in vivo.* We may then proceed to the almost life-size reconstruction of the crime. This is the moment of vivi-experimentation on potentially susceptible animals. But this stage is not necessary if we have been able to establish conviction on the group of preceding cross-checks. Moreover, it is not all that fruitful, either because the animals are not susceptible to human viruses or because the disease that is induced does not have much to do with the disease as it would appear in

---

*AIDS is precisely a state of loss of the immune defenses.

†Most viruses, and particularly that of AIDS, are "silent" a long time in carriers and may reveal themselves by a "disease" only months, even years, later.

humans. Elsewhere, the observation of spontaneous diseases in the animal closely resembling those of humans might ultimately contribute to the establishment of "truth." But biological truth is not the truth of justice. In good scientific logic, the culprit will be held as such, even if, lacking the unlikely proof by quick check,* the amalgam of the facts collected makes the collusion of theoretical virus and isolated virus plausible. "Bio-logic" can be satisfied with these indirect proofs, where what is plausible, compatible, likely, is often adequate. Nonetheless, before deciding as to the responsibility of the suspect, we shall have meticulously checked that no alibi can invalidate the accusation; what scientific procedure must then seek to establish is the impossibility of excluding the designated suspect. This search for negative proof is at least as important as the collection of positive data implicating the suspect.

To find the AIDS virus will be to conduct an investigation in the pure medico-detective tradition which runs without major innovation from Sherlock Holmes to Inspector Colombo; from Pasteur to Dr. Livingstone.

Pitfalls

As is to be expected, the path is strewn with technical and conceptual snares and snags. To establish the presence of the virus on AIDS terrain is uncertain not only because of the techniques which must be employed in doing so. To define AIDS without ambiguity and to establish its world picture are two enterprises of a high degree of uncertainty from the start of the investigation.

How to define AIDS and how to recognize it? It is an apparently new disease. At least for the physicians of the West, it is certainly so. How do we go about describing and baptizing a new disease? By collecting facts—symptoms—which we arrange and classify. The

---

*Innoculation in the susceptible animal of the suspect virus and reproduction on the animal scale of the human disease therafter.

symptoms are, literally, brought to us by the patient: "I don't feel well," "I've lost weight," "I have a fever," "I'm not the way I used to be." Medical questioning will help reveal what might be unaccustomed, on the order of a change, in those who come to consult us. These associated symptoms in the same patient, these groupings of signs of *something wrong,* will permit the outlining of a "syndrome," a group of symptoms. Thus the acquired immune deficiency syndrome is a group of sign-symptoms which bear witness to a collapse of immunity. This collapse has as its consequences the onset of infections due to certain microbes or of a skin cancer—Kaposi's sarcoma. Immune collapse is said to be "acquired" in AIDS, in contrast to collapses of the immune system which certain infants can inherit from their parents.

Physician-clinicians, those who work at the patients' bedside, will have furnished the first descriptive accounts. On the quality and pertinence of these initial notes depended the whole subsequent investigation. As much as possible, it was necessary to circumscribe what *is* AIDS from what *is not.* The difficulty would not be so much to take everything—grippes, colds, eczemas, boils, etc.—for infections of the AIDS type as, specifically, to be able to recognize the infections which authenticate AIDS: *toxoplasms** in the brain, *pneumocystis** in the lungs, *cryptosporidium** in the intestines, etc.—all microorganisms which are sources of infections characteristic of AIDS. This medical "poetics" of microbes is not only phonetically laborious; it is hard to identify incontrovertibly in a given subject who is suffering, one in the brain, another in the lungs or the intestines. The identification of these germs supposes an examination capacity which for the most part is newly accessible. Hence the inaptitude of a fraction of the medical world and, above all, the impossibility of making complete examinations in all parts of the world. A diagnosis of AIDS is difficult in Central Africa—medical testimonies might thereby be afflicted with this primary weakness, which is why, for the synthesizer, the geographical orchestration of

*Micro-organisms which are sources of infections characteristic of AIDS.

AIDS cannot merely accept the "We have no AIDS here," especially since the voice on the telephone wire which makes this statement sometimes follows it, in a still deeper tone, with "and in any case, we have no homosexuals here...." On the other hand, the international ledger of AIDS can enter positive descriptions only provided they satisfy the textbook description. But what is this standard description? Kaposi's sarcoma and/or infections to certain micro-organisms without known causes of breakdown of immunity.

At the University of Vienna in 1872, a Dr. Kaposi described a skin disease characteristic of Mediterraneans, Armenians, Central European Jews, Southern Italians, Corsicans—a rather benign disease, since "survival" was longer than ten, even fifteen, years. So we knew, long before AIDS, a disease bearing, as was customary in the nineteenth century, the name of its discoverer.

Since 1948, long before AIDS, the territory of Kaposi's sarcoma was widened for the first time to include Africa. Dermatologists and then pathologists (those who take a tiny piece of your skin and cut it into ultrathin slices which to their eyes, are transparent, since with the help of a microscope they read the exact diagnosis on these fragments) had clearly recognized the sign "Kaposi" on the skin of many Africans. They also noted that the Kaposi sign covered, in Africa, two apparently different diseases—one related to those of Mediterraneans and not very troublesome (the "indolent" form of Kaposi's sarcoma), the other much less frequent but much more severe, in which lesions are not limited to the skin but affect many organs (glands, lungs, intestines, heart, etc.) and are soon mortal ("aggressive" form of Kaposi's sarcoma).

Since the appearance of AIDS in America and in Europe, the field of Kaposi's sarcoma, a disease hitherto rare in our regions, has considerably widened without our believing it necessary to add the necessary descriptive retouches. So that medical nomenclature does not clearly tell the difference between a case of AIDS with Kaposi's sarcoma and a case of Kaposi's disease without AIDS. Troublesome, since there are cases of Kaposi's sarcoma in *young homosexuals* who nonetheless do not seem to have the dread AIDS. In short, patients who have a limited skin disease ought not be entered in our ledger. This is certainly the case for the vast majority of the "indolent" Kaposi's sarcoma of Africa.

The geographical distribution of AIDS will be one of the elements reported by the investigation. But it is clear that the worldwide AIDS ledger is not near to be drawn up in "indelible ink," for who, and with what means, has ventured into the Brazilian tropical forests to check whether the Indians there are or are not affected? The materiality of the facts in this disease exists only in the eyes of the physician-observers, many of whom are as lacking in AIDS-knowledge as in the long-fiber periscopes, alias fibroscopes,* which can probe the lungs and take samples, for example, of the unknown bacteria (pneumocystis) which is one of the AIDS signatures.

The disease is raging in the USA and has barely shown itself in Europe. The American doctors and biologists should have all the instruments to conduct the investigation by themselves, to its conclusion. It is in the States that molecular biology and radar-probes for discovering viruses have been developed at an incredible rate. It is also in the States that the "human raw material" accumulates at a rate of some 60 (August 1983) new cases per week (more than 100/week in Oct. 1984). Yet the contribution of Parisian physicians could be essential. A simple phenomenon of history the French doctors happen to be at the gates of Africa, with sanitary links to the former colonial territories. They will rapidly inform their transatlantic colleagues that AIDS is present there. Also, they will help to untangle the AIDS-homosexuality imbroglio and its "multi factors" by reporting "from outside" at a distance from this socio-cultural confusion, hetero cases that are not sexual.

---

*Instruments for exploring the natural conduits (intestine, rectum, respiratory trait) constituted of long glass fibers and provided both with a lighting system for "seeing" and an oscillating system for washing and sucking up secretions.

3

ON THE TRAIL OF THE VIRUS

IN JULY 1982, WHEN THE "VIRAL HYPOTHESIS" IS FORMULATED, ON the basis of the available information, it is the "best," and most effective one to clear the AIDS field of the sensational and wild speculations that encumbered it from the start. To discover the AIDS virus will consist, first of all, in collecting, on the terrain of facts, all the signs and indications that describe, limit, characterize, the "new" disease, then constructing with this composite an image-file with which to (re)search in our heads, our books, or our computers which one of the viruses we already know that might correspond to the character thus constructed.

Four areas of raw information suggested themselves to the investigators: geography (where is AIDS found throughout the world?), biology, anatomy (which are the diseased cells and what are the anatomical consequences of disease?), epidemiology (how does the disease spread?).

AIDS Geography: a Disease of Exotic Countries

This assertion appears to contradict the epidemic in the States and the wave of cases in Europe, two regions of the globe where the strange and the exotic are rare enough for us to seek them out, specifically, elsewhere. First of all, the United States and Europe will be withdrawn from our world-accounts, for it is impossible that the disease AIDS could have broken out in these regions and on this epidemic scale before 1980 without having been noticed. So the AIDS virus, whatever it may be, must have been newly introduced among the North American and European populations and must have come from somewhere else, unless we suppose it was created on the spot. This would be a very "costly" hypothesis and, moreover, a totally useless one if we could now account for the history of AIDS without having to invent an entirely new virus. But that it was neither American nor European would not have sufficed to pin the label *exotic* on the AIDS chart. It is a consideration of the map of the world which will have led us to this appellation. An intrinsically fragmentary consideration, but one which will have been no less informative for that, of at least three "centers": Africa, Japan, the Caribbean. Sufficient to justify the label *exotic*.

EQUATORIAL AFRICA

It was in Paris and in Brussels that African AIDS was "discovered." In October 1983, 53 patients of African origin, coming from 8 different countries, had been examined in Paris (18 cases) and in Brussels (35 cases) for serious and repeated infections of those "opportunistic" microbes whose list today is, in and of itself, characteristic of AIDS: pneumocystis carinii, toxoplasma, cryptococci, candida, etc. To these 53 African men and women are added at least 4 Caucasians (white-race subjects of European origin, one of whom was a woman) who had lived in one of these 8 countries of central Africa from which the African patients come: Mali (2 cases), Gabon (2 cases), Ruanda (2 cases), Burundi (1 case), Chad (1 case), Cameroon (1 case), Cape Verde Islands (1 case), Congo-Brazzaville (3 cases), and above all Zaire (40 cases). The average age of these patients is 35 and the proportion of men and women is about 1.5 (32 men, 21 women).

The first patient, however, was not African. He had been seen by a number of Parisian doctors. This was in 1978–1979. Monsieur F., a taxi driver of Portuguese origin, living in Paris since 1976, had on many occasions checked in at the Claude-Bernard Hospital, a center specializing in the diagnosis and treatment of infectious diseases of tropical origin. Monsieur F. had in fact been suffering since 1977 from recurrent infections from the following microbes: pneumocystis carinii (and he had had a serious pneumonia on account of this germ); Candida albicans, a microscopic fungus which he had on his skin and on the mucous membrane of his mouth and throat; papovavirus, responsible for ordinary warts but which, in his case, assumed spectacular proportions (hands, forearms, and legs were covered by an efflorescence of these warts). Finally, in 1979, the hospital identified the presence of multiple abscesses in the brain, a probable infection of "toxoplasm," from which he was to die not long after, upon his return to Portugal. As these numerous infections would suggest, Monsieur F.'s lymphocytes (blood corpuscles representing the immune system) were profoundly abnormal, as much by their extremely reduced number as by their functioning. The disease had apparently begun in 1977 and was to "last" three years, until its fatal outcome. When we had seen him, in 1978, no article and no medical allusion mentioned observations of this type. *A fortiori*, no information circulated publicly as to what would be named AIDS three years later. At the time we had seen him, it was not "unthinkable" that Monsieur F. had contracted a dangerous infection, as yet unknown, of African origin. Monsieur F., a young Portuguese man, had been in the Portuguese navy, in Angola, early in the seventies. Having become, after demobilization in 1973, a truck driver in Angola, he had many times taken the road that crosses a part of Zaire from Angola to Mozambique. When in December 1981 we read the description of AIDS in the American press and the medical journals, it struck us that Monsieur F. and his unfortunate history resembled point by point that of the "new" disease.

During 1982, three other patients were seen in Paris of a description obviously comparable to that of AIDS. All of them (and two were women) had had some link with Africa. One was a black woman living in the Cape Verde Islands, a former Portuguese colony off the Senegalese coast. The other woman was Caucasian and had married a native of Zaire, where she had lived a long time before falling ill. Africa, then—and especially Zaire, three times out of four—recurred in these observations. This African constellation was indicated to the Centers for Disease Control in Atlanta in the course of 1982. Dr. James Curran, head of the AIDS task force, informed us in return of the existence of an AIDS case in West Germany, occurring in an African from Zaire. Moreover, the examination of African medical archives available in Paris produced, between the lines, hints of the probable presence of AIDS in Africa for a long period. We had scoured the medical literature, that of French and Belgian doctors, Africanologists, had studied the medical documents bearing (more or less detailed) records and annotations of African diseases "related to" AIDS.

Now as we saw earlier, there exists at least one—and perhaps several—such diseases. The student of tropical pathology knows Kaposi's sarcoma to be present throughout trans-Saharan Africa. Particularly frequent in Zaire, compared to the neighboring countries, it exists there in two identifiable forms: a "benign" form, by far the most frequent, affecting 10 adult men for each woman, and which probably has little in common with AIDS; a "malign" form, often developing mortal consequences, affecting women and children in the same proportion as men. Now, Kaposi's sarcoma is one of the possible manifestations of AIDS in North America and in Europe; and in fact the AIDS-Kaposi's cases resemble the malign forms of the central African Kaposi's cases. This resemblance concerns the skin disease itself, disseminated and generalized, and its association with multiple microbe infections so characteristic of AIDS in the New World. Books, articles, and theses of Africanologist physicians show some indication as to the presence of AIDS-type infections in Africans suffering from a skin disease of the Kaposi's type. The publications barely antedate 1980. Written in French for the most part, they are not known to most English-speaking doctors.

Elsewhere, specialists had recently been made aware of epidemics of serious infections of cryptococci (a microbe responsible for an infection characteristic of AIDS) in these same regions. We also knew, and for a longer time, the extreme seriousness of certain forms of measles in (otherwise healthy) children and adults, notably in Zaire. (Measles is linked to a viral infection that immune defenses normally limit. We may wonder if these measles in Zaire are so serious precisely by reason of the subjacent or associated infection by the AIDS virus.)

In January 1982, the French experience of AIDS will include Africa as one of the centers of the disease. "An African hypothesis for AIDS" will be the subject of the scientific seminars in which we participated in New York, Boston, and Bethesda, in February 1983. In the course of this same year, several medical articles published in the London *Lancet* will repeat the French observations and confirm the existence of the African focus. It was recalled that a woman surgeon of Danish nationality had succumbed in Denmark to a disease unknown at the time; it would be understood, retrospectively, that this woman, who had practiced in Zaire, had contracted AIDS. This occurred in 1977.

In November 1983, a businessman of about 50 years of age died in Copenhagen after a long series of infections, including a pneumocystis carinii pneumonia (the pneumocystis microbe is responsible for infections characteristic of AIDS). He had lived during 1974 in Ruanda, then from 1976 to 1980 in Burundi. He had also made brief sojourns to the Ivory Coast, Zaire (two days) and Kenya. Since December 1981, he had lived in France and Denmark. He had never had a blood transfusion, had never taken hard drugs intravenously, and did not acknowledge any homosexual experience. How had he contracted AIDS?

The Parisian investigation concerning central Africa will have been consolidated by one conducted quite independently, but concurrently, by Belgian doctors since 1980. The Belgians, whose historical link with Zaire is well known, reported, in the February 1983 *Lancet*, four very well-documented cases of AIDS among men and women of Zaire wealthy enough to leave their country and travel to Belgium for extended treatment in the most renowned hospitals. These were not half-starved, poor, and disinherited Africans who "can contract any disease." The Belgian and French doctors were able to consider, in cooperation, the best means of making known the importance of the African focus—less in round numbers (though there was every reason for thinking that the number of cases in Africa had to be 100 or 1,000 times higher than the number of cases seen in Paris and in Brussels than for its "epidemiological" signification).

The opening of an African trail was to be an important contribution, especially for disentangling the AIDS imbroglio as it was developing in the United States. In contrast to the multifactorial carryall of risks envisaged for North American and European homosexuals—with the disorders of poppers, drugs, sexual overexertion, lotions and creams, contaminated saunas and death-dealing sperm—the African cases (including the French and Danish ones) are almost all quite simple. We find in them none of the risk factors envisaged for and by the North Americans. No homosexuality, no drugs, no transfusions. So we are forced to imagine other modes of transmitting the disease in Africa. This point is crucial. Furthermore, to include Africa in the various AIDS focus of the world is also to rethink the geographical and/or historical origins of the disease. Perhaps might Africa also be its historical source? Or was AIDS exported much earlier? To answer this question would not seek to make Africa responsible for the present Western epidemic (as if one could by rights make a region of the world responsible for bio-historical and geo-climatic local conditions possibly favorable to the survival and proliferation of certain viruses!) Yet an African origin of AIDS would be of great importance for identifying the virus in question.

To rediscover AIDS in Africa was, finally, to cast doubt on the notion of a *new* infectious disease; a doubt supported by the fact, as we have already seen, that the malignant forms of Kaposi's syndrome in Zaire might testify to the long-standing nature of the disease in these regions. On the contrary, we would have great difficulty in imagining that the AIDS-Kaposi's syndrome, observed today in Zaire, would be unrelated to those cases noted in that country since 1948 and even earlier. For virus-hunters—whatever the exact dating of AIDS in Africa—the mere presence of the disease in these regions was a cornerstone for research. The fact is ineluctable: AIDS and its virus are present in Zaire in regions where malignant forms of Kaposi's syndrome are observed.

JAPAN

It was belatedly, almost surreptitiously, that the first Japanese cases of AIDS were announced in July 1983. At this time, two cases were recognized, but several others would be in gestation. The first case concerns a hemophiliac; the other a 40-year-old woman in Shikoku, a southern island of the archipelago. Mrs. W. was a woman "without a history." She had never traveled farther than Kyoto, and was the faithful wife of a decorous husband. A purely autochthonous case of AIDS. Surprising to the medical authorities—to the point where the corridors of medical congresses buzzed with suspicious rumors as to its authenticity. It was necessary to probe the factual bases of this case possibly of a strategic value. This was done at the international meeting at Cold Spring Harbor in September 1983. The Japanese physician who had reported the case under discussion was to explain his reasons for retaining the diagnosis of AIDS in this Shikoku bourgeoise. Reexamination, however, would leave little doubt. It seemed to be an authentic and *local* case of AIDS. In an apparently untroubled region of Japan, in a proper town where the dramas that so often disturb our communities do not occur.

A medical freak, apparently with no relation to AIDS, in this same region of the southwest part of Japan, another disease elsewhere infrequent is widely observed: leukemia of the T-lymphocytes—a disease characterized by multiplication of these cells.* The investigation notes this fact, just in case, in order to be complete, as

---

*The lymphocytes, cells representing immunity, are classifiable into two groups, B-lymphocytes and T-lymphocytes.

is appropriate in any good investigation. AIDS is present in Japan in a region in which leukemias of the T-lymphocytes are observed. Noted.

THE CARIBBEAN

Among the many islands and islets in the Caribbean, some reported cases of AIDS in 1983: Tobago, Dominica, Jamaica, and Martinique. But Haiti occupies a little envied first place—a harsh reality for its nationals—in the absolute number of cases; on the island itself, and among Haitians of the recent diaspora: in the United States, in Canada, in France, in French Guiana, in Germany. It is during 1982 that the hospitals of Miami, New York City, and Newark report to the CDC the AIDS cases of these Haitian men and women, in occasionally tragic circumstances. In August 1982, some 40 patients are thus collected, men and women both. If many of these were poor, there were also some who were well off, of an "upper middle class" social level, according to a sociological scale known only to the United States and the People's Republic of China.

In September 1983, there were 115 cases on record in the USA, 99 men and 16 women of recent Haitian extraction. The population of Haitian refugees in the other countries completed these figures which, added to the intra-island cases, rose to more than 250: men, women, and also a small number of babies. If homosexuality reasonably "explained" a certain number of these male cases, it was inoperative for the rest. The modes of contamination on the island therefore remain mysterious, as much for the natives as for those men and women, resident in Haiti, but of European or North American origin, who have there contracted AIDS.

Monsieur C., a French geologist of about 40 years of age had left Europe in 1978 to live on the island, in the company of a young Haitian woman. Nothing being so lasting in such circumstances but the pains of heartbreak, Monsieur C. returned to his country and his family four years later, under the influence of a "wicked spell" cast upon him by his companion. In the months following his return, he falls gravely ill and dies in Paris in December 1982. Of a cerebral toxoplasmosis, an infection characteristic of AIDS.

Mlle. Y. had taken the veil of the Sisters of Charity and vowed to serve humanity, which she did admirably during long years on the island of Haiti. Toward the end of her apostolate, she abandoned the veil in order to devote herself to the spiritual welfare of the prostitutes of Port-au-Prince, the island's capital. But she falls sick and must leave the island. Hospitalized in Montreal, she will die there of AIDS authenticated by Canadian physicians. She confides to them, before dying, that she had had a single intimate contact with a Haitian man, more than four years before falling ill.

Africa, Japan, the Caribbean: the temporary map of AIDS throughout the world gave us a special image of the disease and of its virus. Was there a link—or links, and which one or ones—between a Zaire diplomat evacuated from Kinshasa to be treated in Brussels, a French engineer working in Haiti, an unadventurous *bourgeoise* from Shikoku, and a homosexual New York disc jockey who has never set foot in Africa? A link other than this unique disease acquired under radically different conditions? To assemble, one way or another, the fragments of what was a biological puzzle might be a decisive means of advancing the investigation as to the identity of the AIDS virus. A virus—at least one—might link all these scattered factors together.

A Disease of the T4-Lymphocytes

Lymphocytes are cells circulating in the blood and the lymph (lymphocyte: cell of the lymph) lodged in lymphatic (or lymphoid) tissues such as the thymus gland, the lymph nodes (alias the "glands"), and the spleen. In lymphocytes considered as a group, we identify a vast subgroup of cells with distinctive characteristics to which the biological lottery has assigned the "number" T4. By means of a simple blood sample, we can separate the lymphocytes from the red corpuscles also present and study their functioning "in culture," in a test tube. We add to the cells certain nutritive elements permitting the lymphocytes not only to survive but also to grow and multiply. In an AIDS victim, the T4-lymphocytes are diseased. Their behavior in culture is deviant. They multiply poorly, produce little, and in the whole perform distinctly less well than the T4-cells belonging to non-AIDS infected individuals.*

The Desert of the Lymphocyte System

The foregoing observations would not suffice to affirm that AIDS is a disease "internal" to the T4-cells, if there were not added to it a very specific anatomical observation. The T4-lymphocytes are here very reduced in number, or even virtually nonexistent. The T4-cells represent nearly two-thirds of the lymphocyte mass in all subjects. They have "vanished" from the blood and tissues of AIDS victims. By the fact of this cellular depopulation, the lymphatic tissues (spleen, thymus, lymph node) habitually provided with T4-lymphoctyes assume a sickly, shrunken, "involuted" aspect. This lymphatic "involution" is characteristic. From these two sources of information— biological and anatomical—the investigation could deduce two hypotheses as to the properties of the virus being sought.

First deduction. If the T4-lymphocytes are diseased, it is because the virus must be or have been present in them. This simple reasoning has many examples in its favor. If grippe is expressed by sneezing, nose-blowing, sore throat, and coughing, it is because the grippe virus "favors" the cells lining the surface of the nose, pharynx, and bronchia. It is here that, as a matter of fact, we find the virus, where it multiplies and reproduces, here in those cells its presence disturbs. The AIDS virus disturbs the T4-cells to the point at which they seem to die of its presence. Starting from this simple construction, we have found a motive for the AIDS virus: it favors

---

*The T4-cells have a major role in immunity. By their presence and the hormones they secrete, they definitely limit the natural expansion of microbes present in most individuals.

the T4-lymphocytes in which it lives and probably multiplies. The AIDS virus must therefore be a "lymphophile" virus, which frequents lymphocytes of a certain type. A virus said to have a T4-tropism (T4-tropic virus).

Second deduction. If the passage of the AIDS virus leaves behind (or with) it this characteristic "wasting" of the lymphocyte cells, it is because the virus, directly or indirectly, involves one or the other of the two following processes: the T4-cells are destroyed to excess even as they are formed (the virus induces a destruction-process of the T4-cells); the T4-cells are no longer formed when they are normally destroyed (the virus induces an a-regeneration process of the T4-cells*). Destruction and/or a-regeneration, the two processes are not mutually exclusive.

The Mysteries of Propagation

THROUGH THE BLOOD

Monsieur D. set out in 1978 to fulfill his national service obligations, and to do so reported to Port-au-Prince, Haiti, as a government administrator. He was accompanied by his young wife and their daughter. A few months later he had a traffic accident on a Haitian highway. Taken in serious condition to the Port-au-Prince hospital, he had to be operated on immediately. His case justified an immediate transfer to a Martinique hospital. He required many transfusions. Eight units of blood recently taken from native volunteers had been prepared for him, and out of the eight he received six, it appears, before his helicopter transfer to Martinique. This occurred in September 1978. He recovered from the accident and

---

*The T4-cells, like lymphocytes in general, are in a state of permanent renewal: the "adult" cells live only a few days to a few months, and the daily contingent of old and subsequently eliminated cells is replaced by an equivalent contingent of "young" cells, these born from the multiplication of the mother cells which form stocks in the re-formation bank which is the bone marrow; the stock-cells of bone marrow are in a constant process of division and compensate for the natural tendency of the cell-type to die out. The T4-cell maintains itself, from stock cells to its descendants, by the daily generation of new T4-cells. A-regeneration is the privation of generation.

seemed to be in good health until February 1982, when there appeared the first signs of what was gradually to reveal itself as a case of AIDS. Four years later! The only event capable of being at the origin of this disease, henceforth recognized as transmissible from one human being to another, was blood; lacking other causes (no homophile sexuality, no drugs), the only rational explanation was contamination by an "exotic virus" carried by the transfusions of blood. Lymphocytes of Monsieur D.'s blood had been sampled before his death. Preserved by refrigeration in a container of liquid (at –170° C), they were transferred, in sealed ampoules, by plane from Paris to the NIH in Maryland. The thawed lymphocytes were then put into a lab culture. A few weeks later, a special virus was discerned in the cultivated lymphocytes, an exotic virus* resembling one widespread among populations of African descent in the Caribbean islands. Four years after the transfusions, Monsieur D.'s blood donors were all traced by the CDC. All eight were in apparently good health.

While the drama of this young Frenchman was taking place, the United States announced the case of a baby given a blood transfusion at birth and contracting AIDS during the following months. The blood donor himself was incubating the disease, from which he died several months later. Since these events, some 70 similar cases have been noted, and for all of them, one or several blood transfusions have been the only factor capable of explaining the appearance of AIDS.

In the course of the year 1982, we became aware of 3, then 5, then 10, cases of hemophiliacs† in whom the same infectious and lymphocyte symptoms have developed as those observed in homosexuals afflicted with AIDS: serious microbic infections normally not dangerous, even harmless. The hemophiliac victims are mostly boys under 12. They have no link—familial or otherwise—with homosex-

---

*We shall have occasion to return to this virus and its relations with the suspect one.

†The hemophiliac inherits through his "carrier" mother (in good health and in every case exempt from the hemorrhaghic accidents of her hemophiliac sons) a genetic anomaly: the absence of "factor VIII" in the blood; this defect involves profound disorders of coagulation.

uals. After many confrontations and discussions, the evidence was incontrovertible. The hemophiliacs' disease was identical in all points to that identified in the homosexuals. How had these boys caught AIDS? Without a doubt by the intermediary of blood or of coagulant fractions which hemophiliacs receive in great quantity.*

SYRINGES AND AIDS

In New York City, a growing number of young drug users, both men and women, are AIDS victims. All use "hard" drugs, which they inject intravenously. This group represents a considerable number of patients: 312 men and 76 women, altogether 388 cases by September 12, 1983. The drug victims are in the process of gradually "catching up" with the homosexual "contingent." The latter has shifted, from January 1982 to September 1983, from 96 percent to 71 percent of the total number of cases declared in the United States, while those using drugs represented at first 3 percent then 17 percent. There are not, to the present time, French cases of AIDS among the users of intravenous drugs. How did the contamination of the North American heroin addicts come about? The process was most likely as follows: a small number of homosexuals, among the first afflicted, were also drug addicts—not more than 5 percent. Now, among heroin addicts, it is common to exchange the instruments used for the dose. Convivially enough, but hygienically to the worst effect. The syringes and needles are summarily rinsed, never enough to neutralize fluids of the preceding user. The virus will be there and will be inoculated into the following user. Henceforth, drug users' AIDS will be only a special case—disturbing by reason of its increase—of the transmission of AIDS through the blood.

MOTHER AND CHILD

To this day, more than 50 babies have died in the 6 months following their birth, with all the signs of a disease identical to AIDS

---

*In order to compensate for their inherited defect, hemophiliacs receive fractions of plasma from donors with normal coagulation. These are the coagulant fractions enriched in so-called factor VIII.

in adults. The mothers are women likely to have encountered the AIDS agent in one way or another. The women from Zaire or Haiti are most often in apparently good health. The other mothers are either drug users themselves or the wives of drug users, or women whose male partner is bisexual. Contamination of the child by the AIDS agent could occur at various moments—in pregnancy, in childbirth, or even, theoretically, in the course of post natal breast-feeding. But it is certainly in the course of the pregnancy itself, *in utero* or at delivery, that the contamination is effected, through the placenta.*

In Paris, in September 1983, two babies were discovered to have contracted AIDS. One mother was from Haiti, the other from Zaire. Since then, at least 5 more cases of AIDS in babies have been known.

Aside from the sociological consequences of the transmission of AIDS through the blood or its derivatives, what have we learned from these transfusional or hemophiliac cases? The agent can be found in the blood of its "carrier." It is here that we must find the virus responsible, if this is technically possible; the virus takes time before manifesting itself in the organism, before showing itself by a disease, AIDS, a humanly unavoidable event, belated, occurring three, even four, years after the infecting inoculation. This period of time is variable, much shorter among babies (a few months at maximum) than among adults receiving transfusions (up to five years). This difference indicates an increased susceptibility of a baby's T-lymphocytes to infection by virus X—a characteristic which suggests that the virus benefits from the state of immune agitation of a newborn baby, whose lymphocytes are literally assailed by the chemical "strangenesses" of the extrauterine world.

But what does the virus do during the long interval when it is present in the organism until the first signs of the disease appear? It is possible that it produces its effects on the T4-lymphocytes very slowly. But we can also envisage that it "shelves itself" in some cellular corner and bides its time. Let us not forget that retroviruses

---

*Area of blood exchange between the mother and her fetus, the placenta is expelled at birth.

can lodge in a segment of chromosome and remain dormant during generations of cells.

Finally we will have learned that the AIDS virus can be carried by *healthy* subjects. All the blood donors used by Monsieur D. were in good health, four years after giving blood.

It will remain to be explained how a virus can be without effect on one subject and the source of disease—"pathogenic"— for another. Similarly, how can it be explained that the blood of a healthy carrier of the hepatitis B virus can be the source of sometimes extremely serious hepatitis in the subject who has received the blood of this healthy carrier? The example of the heptatitis B virus is here to remind us that these questions are not new ones and that we know practically nothing about the mechanisms that determine events so different. We know nothing, or almost nothing, outside of empirical observation. A subject Y, carrier of a virus X, is healthy; Y's blood is given to Z, who will die of the infection from virus X. This is the riddle. Might it be a matter of some patients' resistance to particular viruses? There are in animals, and for various microbes, some resistant stocks, and others which are susceptible, but there is no human "stock" so homogeneous. Might it be a question of a subtle modification of the virus itself, occurring during its "passage" from one subject in which it was harmless to another where it becomes pathogenic? This is a possibility. The passage of a virus from one "species" to another has occasionally been marked by minor modifications of the virus's structure: mouse virus to monkey virus; monkey virus to human virus. But here we are remaining within the human species. Might it be a matter of an association of malignant viruses: one + one = AIDS? Certain "defective" viruses (viruses unable to replicate) find in a partner-virus the means of producing *á deux* what they could not have done alone. Like the blind man and the paralytic.

AIDS AND SEXUALITY

The least we can say is that propagation by sexuality exists and in a manner more than reasonably documented. Nonetheless Masters and

Johnson, in this matter, have had no cause to furnish us their opinions. Indeed, beyond the word "sexual," we have few details. We might speak quite as allusively of "highly intimate contacts" without further effect. This evasive qualification says nothing about sexual contacts and their variety. Which is certainly too bad, and even extremely serious, if we seek to help exposed people to protect themselves during intimate contacts. With regard to prevention, it would be much more effective to specify which "gestures" are really dangerous, rather than to ban sexuality altogether. In June 1982 the CDC reports the first chain transmissions of AIDS among groups of homosexual men. Each link of the chain is represented by individual patients related to one another by one or several intimate encounters. Most spectacular (and demonstrative), one of these chains of transmission of disease clustered 40 cases, from the Pacific to the Atlantic, with mini-branches in Miami, Chicago, and elsewhere—40 cases, all intersecting, directly or not, with one and the same distributor, an AIDS patient, who was the source of several mini-chains of contamination. An exemplary, if caricatural, case that establishes the reality of intimate transmission, the activism of certain individuals, its infectious and contagious danger.*

Homosexuality = sodomy? So rumor has it. A certain number of women have contracted the disease with, for the sole risk factor acknowledged, that of being or having been the partners of men who were drug users or bisexual. These women have declared, insofar as they have been willing to speak frankly to Centers for Disease Control agents, that they have been contaminated in the absence of any sodomitic activity. This indicates, assuming their testimony is valid, that intimate contacts, of whatever nature, between a woman and a man affected by or carrying the agent can be the source of contamination for that woman. As of early 1984,

---

*Activism in no way prejudices the literally active or passive position of the subjects concerned. No quantitative information exists on this point of primary importance, for if there were no AIDS subject among the exclusively active subjects, we might have learned a great deal, notably as to the "retrograde" noncontagiosity of the virus. Yet it has not been possible to answer clearly on this point. Nonetheless, it appears that passive subjects are more vulnerable to contamination than active ones.

woman-to-man transmission of AIDS through intimate (sexual) contacts could not be clearly documented. However, the Africa-connected cases noted in Europe, and later in Zaire itself, suggested it was quite possible. Indeed, nearly as many women as men are afflicted there. In the U.S., few women have contracted the disease, thus restricting the probability that they would themselves have "a chance" to contaminate an occasional male partner. These negative observations could still indicate that the AIDS agent is unequally transmitted—men to women, indeed—and this definitively has been established, but not "so readily" from women to men. If true, this asymmetry of propagation could in part explain the observed confinement of AIDS in the so-called risk groups during the early years of the epidemics.

So, homosexual men stricken with AIDS number several orders of magnitude greater than afflicted women. Would this simplistically reveal some mysterious "intrinsic" resistance of women to sodomitic risk (!) or to invasion of their body by the AIDS agent? Some surveys have revealed that at least 20 percent of women under 40 have or have had "unnatural relations," as the French law still stipulates (*contra-naturam*), with their male sexual companion(s). Increasing numbers of women are coming down with AIDS also. More realistically, if women have seemed relatively protected from AIDS, might it not have reflected their rarer engaging into sex, whether orthodox or atypical, with homosexual men than the said men do among themselves? What distinguishes the stricken homosexuals is the number of average intimate partners they disclose. We know the figures given for the United States: the record is situated at around 1,000 per year, and the "median" around 78.

And prostitutes? A few New York prostitutes have been stricken, but only a few (January 1984). Is this again a testimony for an intrinsic resistance of women, related to some refractory impermeability of the vaginal mucous membrane? Here we are carried to the realm of ghosts and fantasies. Would it not be simpler to assume that the number of polygamous homosexuals who also offer their attentions to the ladies is limited? But then American homosexuals would have been the primary source of the American disease. On this point, the historical record is without ambiguity. The first American victims were, as we all know, almost all male homosexuals.

As we see, the empirical and statistical observations leave us uninformed. So much for the voyeur who would like to employ them for his own projections as for those seeking a clarified comprehension, one that is biologically real, of AIDS-transmission during intimate contacts. Let us proceed differently. Since transmission through blood is more clearly understood, it is from such understanding that more pertinent deductions might be drawn.

Since the virus seems to require lodging in lymphocyte cells, we shall follow the path of the lymphocytes. Where, outside of the blood and the internal lymphoid organs, are these cells found? In the external secretions: a little in the normal saliva, a little in the vaginal secretions (outside of menstrual periods or a genital infection), a little in urine. Distinctly more in the sperm. The virus, then, might be transmitted by the intermediary of infected lymphocytes and deposited on a mucous membrane. In order to be infected by the AIDS virus, then, it would be necessary to "receive" these carrier cells, and they would then have to be put in contact with the host's lymphocytes. The sperm's lymphocytes, even when infected by the AIDS virus, are not spermatozoa. They are not endowed with that tail whose rapid reptatory movements give the spermatozoa seen under a microscope such extreme mobility. The spermatozoa rush past; the lymphocytes loiter in one spot. They are incapable of making the long trajectories covered by the indefatigable spermatozoa. Consequently, we must assume that inoculation of the AIDS virus by means of the lymphocytes would imply a direct or quasi-direct contact of the donor's lymphoctyes with those of the recipient. *I.e.,* this cannot occur by shaking hands with a virus-carrier, nor by drinking out of your neighbor's glass, nor by kissing that neighbor on his (her) cheek. During sexual relations between males, the inoculation would occur all the more "effectively" if there were direct contact between the "carrier" lymphocytes and the capillary vessels on the surface of the recipient's mucous membranes. Doctors specializing in rectoscopies* instruct us in this regard: the rectal mucous membrane is particularly fragile when there is, on this level, an inflammation. In this case, the mere contact of the mucous membrane with the rigid rectoscope is an immediate factor of a mini-erosion without any danger except that it opens micro-lakes of blood in which the examinee's blood (and the lymphocytes contained in it) can henceforth make contact with the "exterior world." "To deposit" lymphocytes carrying a virus X in these places and conditions would be an occasion of contamination of the recipient. In this deductive bio-logical scenario, the scene would be equivalent to a "mini-transfusion" upon contact with the abraded mucous membrane.

IN THE TROPICS: INSECTS AND SYRINGES

Sex and blood, blood and/or sex, we have not thereby exhausted the questions which must be asked apropos of transmission. Some mysteries remain on this point in Haiti and Africa: for a number of AIDS cases seen in Europe, having lived a "normal" (heterosexual) life in the three to four years preceding disease in these tropical regions is the sole factor that distinguishes these male and female patients from those seen in the U.S. The question of contamination comes up particularly unanswered at first for those men whose exclusive heterosexuality cannot be in doubt. They have not received blood transfusions nor introduced needles or drugs into their veins. How could the AIDS virus, which is not contagious through air and is not transmitted during casual contacts, have penetrated the body of these men in these regions (assuming that women there would have been infected through hetero-sex)? Theoretical explanations can be proposed, plain heterosexual contacts being first. As indicated previously, cases related to Africa number as many women as men. More factually, a survey conducted in the fall of 1984 in Kinshasa, Zaire, has revealed cases of AIDS among different men clustering around one single woman. Similar groupings of cases also have been documented in service men in the U.S.A. Thus it appears that

---

*Inspection of the rectum by means of an instrument furnished with an optical system.

transmission (presumably through sex) could be transitive to both sexes, although some quantitative asymmetry remains a possibility: more readily from men to women than vice-versa. If confirmed, the asymmetry of intimate propagation would be of great importance to the prospects of the epidemic and its limitations. At the same time, it would outline an additional silhouette to the searched virus.

Besides sex and transfusion, AIDS-virus inoculation could also occur through the skin by *injection*—through insect bites or needle punctures. In tropical regions, a whole series of viruses and parasites can be transmitted by the bites of carrier insects. The most classic is the agent of malaria, "plasmodium." But there are many others, notably yellow fever and other AR-BO viruses, so called because they are *ar*thropod-borne, carried by special insects. The common bedbug once regained its titles of nobility, becoming *cimex hemipterus,* thanks to a Nobel prize winner's text which proved the presence of the virus of hepatitis B in the body of these nasty creatures, guests of certain hotels in the city of Dakar. Tropical Africa, and notably its jungle and humid regions, swarms with all the insect fauna that could be desired. The scenario of the events of interhuman contamination is virtually always the same, to the last nuance: a stinging insect takes blood from a first contaminated victim and proceeds to regurgitate it into the blood of a second victim. It would be necessary, in order to satisfy our conditions for the transmission of AIDS, that the vector-insect thus transfer certain contaminated lymphocytes from one subject to the other. There exists still another hypothesis. This one much more human.

In Africa, in the 1960's, in Zaire in particular, "decolonization" is the rule, and the Belgians are on the way out. They take little enough wealth with them, but all their knowhow. In the hospitals, their departure is tangible: as much on the nursing level as on that of the training of the doctors. Supplies are no longer so sterilely handled. But the syringes were made then of glass. And the nursing personnel broke many of them. The useful life of a syringe was thereby shortened all the more. The risks of passing on to one what might have been taken from another was thereby reduced. But a great

sanitary disaster never arrives singly. Deliveries of disposable supplies began in the mid 1970's. In chronic penury: not enough syringes or needles for everyone, but all disposable. Plastic, indestructible,
unbreakable supplies, unsterilizable by the usual means—and indefi-
nitely *reusable*. The weapon of the crime so honed and polished, the
motives could be found in emergency or convenience, for instance.
And we can imagine the scene in which the medical orderly announces to the community of the hospitalized or of the consultants:
"Everyone standing at the foot of his bed, we shall begin *the*
injection." The same for everyone. Or again, the lure of petty profit,
in cash or in fame. In order to round out the skimpiness of the days'
receipts, take flasks containing the remains of the therapeutic manna,
for instance white penicillin; visit the villages in order to give the
sufferers a saving or symbolic injection. With the same syringe!
Then no more would be needed than one "carrier" during the visit,
and we are back to the transmission of AIDS by syringe and needle,
whose effectiveness we have already learned from the drug addicts.

The (not-so-ancient) history of medicine swarms with precedents
of this type, in which the transmission of infectious agents is caused
by the intermediary of treatment. In Africa* or elsewhere. Didn't
the infectious hepatitis now assigned to virus B used to be called
"syringe hepatitis"? And even before disposable syringes, weren't
"local" epidemics observed in Africa after the installation of Western-
type humanism in the form of missionary hospitals? Medicine has
long since made a name for itself out of these therapeutic boo-boos
in which it participates: *nosocomial* (from the Greek root *nosocomios*
= hospital). The mysterious part of the transmission of the AIDS
virus in Africa might thus be only a riddle concerning three needles
but only two syringes, in which the secrets of contamination would
be yielded up in the form of such paramedical blunders. Such
"episodes" do not happen only to other people, nor only in Africa,
nor only to human beings. Cattle too have long suffered from the
touching attentions of the veterinarian missionaries of prophylaxis.†

---

*See page (21), the section devoted to the new viruses.
†The virus of bovine leukemia, frequent in European livestock, is regularly transmitted during
vaccination sessions with a single syringe.

What about AIDS transmission in Haiti? Was Sister Y., whom we have already described, a late victim of her own humanly fall or was she stricken by a divine scourge? Bitten by a bedbug in one of those dubious hotels which her vocation obliged her to visit? Or was she, too, a victim of that paramedical tradition which consists in giving yourself an injection of vitamin C, of vitamin B-12, of aspirin, or of wonder drugs? Is not the country swarming with voodoo priests (one for every hundred inhabitants)? They take over "traditional medical practice," which resorts to methods at once ancient and modern; a mixture in which we find the *piqû,* a creole word that nicely puts what we mean: puncture and injection. Here too, the (plastic) tragedy of the unsterilizable syringes might have played its part.

The disease AIDS thus located, identified, characterized, its modes of propagation on the record, investigators of the medico-biological Interpol could get to work.

4

TYPICAL PORTRAIT: RESEARCH PROCEDURES

FOUR PARTICULARS MAKE THE AIDS VIRUS A REMARKABLE VIRO-logical being. First of all, its target. By choice the AIDS virus affects and infects special cells, themselves specialized: the T4-lymphocytes. Second, its effects. A T4-virus—lymphophile but cunning. The T4's affected will die without growing back. After the virus sets in, a lymphocyte desert appears. Third, its interhuman propagation. The lymphophile virus, "devouring" T4's, is transmitted by blood and by sexual intercourse, from man to man or from man to woman. Finally, its geography. Africa, Japan, the Caribbean. An exotic virus, perhaps as old as Africa and which, starting from that continent, has made a world tour. T4-trope, hemo-sexual, tropical—a very special virus indeed.

This four-point description will keep us from fixing our sights too long on abusive suspects eager for notoriety, or those we might have found in the patient but that have come upon the scene of the crime after the lymphocyte shop window has been broken by someone else.

The central file of killer viruses does not appear on the computer. If the computer is mute, the "mug shots" of some are clear and complete. And it is from the human mind that recognition will leap forth. Better than computers— as they are operated or programmed by men—the mind uses everything at once: analogical resemblance ("the relationship of two or more things that offer among themselves a certain community of features") we can look for analogies even in (and including) antinomic reversals; inference, a logical operation "by which we admit a proposition by virtue of its links with other propositions already held to be true"; induction, which "consists in proceeding from singular and special phenomena to a more general proposition"; and many other mental operations.

Which among the humanophiliac viruses might adhere to the typical portrait we were able to establish? In truth, none! None which without major retouching could fulfill all the requisite conditions. Especially not the cytomegalovirus (CMV—infecting extremely various kinds of cells whose nucleus it causes to enlarge) which had initially proposed itself as a candidate. We can measure, today, in the history of the search for a virus, the value of the initial propositions in favor of one of the oldest viruses of the Old World and the New. Of course, its dossier contained its "titillations" of the immune system and the little jolts it appeared to give the T4-lymphocytes. But the CMV has never led all by itself to that total lymphocyte "evacuation," the absolute sign of the AIDS virus; always present in us* we would have to assume that a mysterious "mutant" stock had surfaced, an aberrant stock, a bastard born of illicit loves, or fruit of some bacteriological warfare. Without such hypotheses having explained how this mutant, supposedly generated in North America or in the Caribbean, had simultaneously managed to distribute itself in Zaire and in Japan. Moreover, no mutant has been found. How many lab mice will have learned the cost of this early affabulation?

Here we are with an AIDS specification and no known virus to take the place indicated. In particular, the devastation of the lymphocyte landscape in subjects who have succumbed to AIDS reveals the presence of the virus X. Impossible to mistake it for any other. This description might well have joined those encyclopedic cata-

---

*At least three fourths of the *healthy* adults of the French population are carriers of the CMV without perceptible harm, and this throughout their entire lives.

logues which contain the unexplained observations of medicine had it not been "rescued" by a cross-check born of a major detour. No human virus, you say, but an animal virus?

Feline AIDS

It was from Cambridge, Massachusetts, that the "news" came. A team of researchers at Harvard's School of Public Health announces in May 1983 the analogy between human AIDS and the AIDS of ... cats! In the 1970's, British and American research workers, independently and then together, had observed and described a deadly lymphocyte anemia in domestic cats. In a kitten's life, the disease is expressed by weight loss, deterioration in general condition, fever, and deadly infections from various microbes, particularly "toxoplasma." A parasite normally harmless in the alley cats where it is commonly found. Moreover, it is cats which, for man, are one of the "reservoir centers" of toxoplasma. Cats, like human beings, normally accommodate themselves to the presence of this parasite, which cannot multiply by reason of the "control" which the T-lymphocytes exert against it. The T-lymphocyte system in cats suffering from lymphocyte anemia is totally defective. Autopsy reveals a major lymphocyte aplasia,* especially marked on the level of the thymus† Lymphatic involution and infection from endogenous germs: so much for the human-cat analogy. At this point we know nothing more than we already knew about human AIDS. AIDS = lymphocyte aplasia and consequent infections.

But in the cat, we knew the virus responsible. Lymphocyte anemia is a disease transmissible by a catalogued virus, a certain virus of feline leukemia (FeLV). In this FeLV, cats have a dread natural predator capable of leading the T-lymph system to its desolation, in the manner of human AIDS. The cell-targets preferred by the feline

---

*Aplasia: incomplete or interrupted development of a tissue or an organ.

†The thymus gland is a lymphatic organ especially developed in young cats. It is "filled" with T-lymphocytes. In human adults of AIDS age, the thymus is normally partially involuted.

virus are the T-lymphocytes. Isolated and characterized around 1975, FeLV is a retrovirus of the family of viruses easily enabled by their chemical makeup to "return" to the chromosomes of the cell on which they are parasites. What are FeLV's effects on the carrier cell? As with most retroviruses, FeLV multiplication involves few cell destructions when it is cultivated *in vitro* with its target cells. How, then, is the AIDS-type lymphocyte aplasia produced in the "whole" cat? A pertinent question, for if we could answer it, we would have a model of the possible effects of the human virus (whatever it might be) on the lymphocyte system. An impertinent question, since we cannot supply a precise answer, only a few vague hypotheses: Might the retrovirus, inserted into the T-cell chromosome, "perturb" its functions, leading to the premature "aging" of the carrier cell? Work on the FeLV virus and its effects on the lymphocyte cells must be continued. In this natural infection there will be certain lessons of the first importance if we are to understand the AIDS-like mechanisms by which a retrovirus works on the lymphocytes.

But FeLV is not the agent of human AIDS. Even if it can infect, under certain conditions, human lymphocytes in cytoculture, FeLV has never been responsible for any infection in "whole" human being, *in vivo*. Feline AIDS is an excellent example for the human variety, but it has its differences from "ours." The first is FeLV's high contagiosity among cats. The virus lodges in the nose and throat of the carrier animals—it infects other cells besides lymphocytes—and is transmitted by licking. The second difference is so radical that the cat "model" thereby seems initially preposterous, even totally incongrous: FeLV, as its name unambiguously shows, is a leukemia virus. Leukemia *and* AIDS—where are we?

Let us take a group of kittens, and inoculate them with a certain dose of FeLV virus. Some of the kittens will show nothing special. Others—the majority—will develop signs of feline AIDS with the characteristic lymphatic aplasia. Finally, a small number will show signs of leukemia: considerable multiplication of the T-lymphocytes of which the total number in the organism and in the blood will have increased at least ten-fold. Why? Because the FeLV retrovirus will have "transformed" certain lymphocytes into cancerous cells endowed with abnormal capacities for multiplication; in principle it suffices for one cell to be thus "transformed" in order to give birth to millions and then billions of "daughter" cancerous cells, all issuing from the first "transformed" cell. A leukemia is really the opposite of AIDS. AIDS is, perhaps, an arrest of normal cell multiplication, resulting in the involution of the lymphatic organs. A leukemia is an accelerated multiplication of "transformed" cancerous cells and the inflation of the number of cells in the lymphatic organs and in the blood. The same type of retrovirus injected into ordinary cats is therefore capable of producing phenomena as contrary as an AIDS-aplasia or a hyperplasia-leukemia.*

Whatever the detailed and molecular explanation of this biological hocus-pocus may be, the fact remains and it is of a great informative importance: AIDS might be a leukemia that has changed its sign: leukemia, +, AIDS,—.

What is true of the cat and of its leukemic virus might also be true of other "leukemic" viruses. Let us return to the file of virus descriptions, this time with leukemia for our second key word. Leukemia and virus—the list is long, the harvest of scientific references copious, to the point of indigestion.

Certain series of viruses, and notably retroviruses, are associated in mice and chickens with cancerous diseases of the blood cells. We also find here certain indications of the alternative, aplasia-leukemia, but for cells other than the lymphocytes—the red cells, for instance. This avalanche of para-analogous animal situations, if it confirmed the model's general validity, does not help us much for AIDS. Let us reformulate our question by putting lymphocyte leukemia side by side with viruses in humans. This time, we get only two answers. The most evident, since the longest-known, concerns certain malignant tumors sometimes accompanied by leukemias, frequent in Af-

---

*Another disease transmissible from animal to animal with this "two-faced" aspect, leukemia or aplasia, has just been described in the monkeys of a New England research center. As leukemia, the monkeys produce a disease of proliferating cells (lymphocytes); as aplasia, other monkeys, injected with extracts of tumors, will produce a disease of the AIDS type.

rica, in regions densely abounding in a virus known as Epstein-Barr virus, the agent in our climates of a nonmalignant disease, infectious mononucleosis. The E-B virus prefers to infect lymphocytes of the "other" category, B-lymphocytes.*

The B-cell-leukemia—E-B virus model—was, of course, interesting, especially since it gives rise, exceptionally, to pseudo-aplasias of the B-lymphocytes. But this is a model quite remote from the T-lymphocytes of AIDS.

The second answer to the leukemia and human virus question. Yes there was another virus, but.... But we had our suspect! It satisfied all the conditions *except* that it is leukemic. After the detour among feline AIDS and the leukemia virus, this difference, leukemia-aplasia, is precisely the *link of contraries.* The record of human viruses contained the detailed description of a leukemia virus of the T-lymphocytes. Study of its file showed us immediately that it was close to the one we had described without knowing it, the one whose robot-portrait has been drawn without knowing that it had almost a "double," already known and repertoried, a virus so to speak copied from the one we were looking for. This time the premium for knowledge and for progress would be worth the obstacles we were holding a suspect. Our task: to prove it guilty or else to exonerate it. Its name HTLV, "Human T-Cell Leukemia Virus."

---

*Lymphocytes as a whole are separable into two subgroups, B-lymphocytes and T-lymphocytes.

· 5 ·

AIDS, SIGNED HTLV?

Who Is HTLV?

HTLV IS A RETROVIRUS. IT IS SUPPLIED WITH AN ENZYMATIC SUB-
stance (the REverse TRanscriptase enzyme, see Chapter 2, page 12)
which permits it to be inserted "back" in the heart of the cell, the
chromosomes, where the information is concentrated which controls
the cell's functioning. The retrovirus HTLV insinuates itself into the
nucleus of the host cell by inserting into it its own nucleic acids. If
the insertion is placed in a "critical" region of the cellular program
the cell's functioning can be radically perturbed by it: "transformation" into a cancerous cell occurs. The "transformed" cell multiplies
incessantly and rapidly into thousands, millions, even billions of
daughter cells, invading the tissues and the blood.

But infection by the HTLV virus is not invariably cancerigenic.
Quite the contrary. The great majority of individuals carrying this
virus in the world are not at all affect ˙ by it, at least in appearance.
These healthy HTLV-carriers are two to three *thousand* times more
numerous than leukemic victims. It is likely that, in these cases, the
"integrated" HTLV remains at a distance from the critical zones* of

---

*These "topological" considerations have merely a hypothetical value, insofar as we do not know
precisely the critical sites of cancerigenic insertion.

cancerization. With time, as the number of intrachromosomic HTLV "copies" increases, the probability of cancerous perturbations also increases. The virus's presence in a carrier is in the long run a risk factor* of the appearance of a leukemia. And the more widespread the virus in a population, the more frequent the leukemia in question.

Cancer, leukemia: What are their relations with AIDS? Those we have found between AIDS, feline leukemia, and the FeLV virus. A single *type* of retrovirus in cats is capable of inducing a cancerous transformation (leukemia) or an aplastic transformation (AIDS). The feline precedent authorized us to agree that a leukemic virus might be involved in human AIDS. Let us therefore continue the reading of the HTLV file.

HTLV is a "new" virus. It is the first and, till now, the only one of the retroviruses which we have never been able to isolate significantly in human cells. It was discovered only at the end of the 1970's, since until then it was not known how first to cultivate the carrier cells. The instrument of this important discovery for medical biology had to wait for certain advances in cytoculture† and, specifically, for the production of a biological fertilizer necessary to the artificial multiplication of the carrier cells: the growth factor‡ of the T-lymphocytes—Interleukine II.

T-Lymphocytes, Targets of HTLV

The HTLV virus has a predilection for cells of the blood and the lymph organs which we have seen constituted the bed and board of the AIDS virus. In its "leukemic form," the only disease for which it is responsible in any established fashion, HTLV gives rise to a cancerization of the T4-lymphocytes. Further, the T4-lymphocytes,

---

*The same considerations apply to liver cancers in relation to the virus of hepatitis B.

†Cell culture in the laboratory.

‡The growth factor, like the virus HTLV, was discovered in a single laboratory in Bethesda, Maryland, by the research unit studying the biology of experimental tumors, directed by Dr. Robert Gallo.

infected by the virus, produce abnormal behavior in cytoculture: sometimes "immortal," animated by uninterrupted divisions and multiplications so long as they are supplied with nutritive elements; sometimes "broken down," aberrant in their biological productions. T-cells infected by HTLV can thus "shift" from a normal function to a quasi-inverse activity. The HTLV virus radically affects the biological behavior of the T-cells it infects.

T4-lymphophiliac and perverse, this description was that of the suspect AIDS. But let us wait for the data of geography. On the map of the globe, HTLV leaves the dotted line of its visits to AIDS sites around the world.

The HTLV Virus in the World

The West Indies and the Antilles, delivered to the appetite of the Western nations, divided up among those peoples and rulers that had the means to send a slave ship out to sea, the Caribbean islands will have been, for the New World, the cradle of HTLV. Here the virus is "associated" with a rare form of leukemia in which the multiplying cells (specifically the T4-lymphocytes) are lodged in the lymphatic ganglia and in the blood. Leukemia, *i.e.,* white (leuco) cells in great number in the blood (hemia), and also, in and under the skin.* But leukemia is a relatively rare consequence of infection by the HTLV virus. The great majority of "carriers" are apparently healthy, and the virus is present† in them without any signs but biological ones. Jamaica, Trinidad, Dominica, St. Vincent, Tobago, the Virgin Islands, Martinique, Désirade, Haiti. The incidence of the "healthy carrier condition" in these regions reaches or exceeds several units per hundred inhabitants. Nearby Central America, Surinam, and the coast of Colombia, also harbor sites of HTLV endemic.

---

*Physicians give this skin disease the name "Sezary," after the dermatologist who recognized in it an analogous form in Europe.
†Discernible in an individual by the antibodies his immune system has produced (see Finding the Agent, page (32).

AIDS, Signed HTLV?

A dozen time zones from Haiti, at 150° longitude, antipodes of the Caribbean, in a subtropical region, the density of HTLV "portage" is even higher. The site happens to be in Japan. What unexpectedly emerges from the HTLV presence in Japan is both the concentration of carrier-individuals in a single region and the parceling out of the virus centers within the endemic zone. Thus at satellite range we observe that the highest "virus" density is inscribed at the southern and western extremity of the country in two large islands (see map on page 50) Kyushu and Shikoku. Kyushu and, in particular, its harbor regions: Kagoshima in the south and Nagasaki in the west, the smaller islands off Kagoshima—Okinawa and Tanegashima—Hirado and Hakate to the north, facing the Straits of Korea and Funaī-Oita to the northeast, facing the Uwajima region on the neighboring island of Shikoku. Shikoku is wedged between Kyushu to the west and the coast region of Kobe-Osaka to the north. Osaka is one of the rare, "continental" regions where the incidence of healthy carriers of HTLV reaches a high figure (4 percent). The rest of Japan is virtually unscathed by the virus, except the region of Yamagushi in the extreme west of "Continental" Honshu.

As our hypothetical satellite approaches land, at about 10 kilometers from the ground, we notice a dispersal in the densities of the carrier populations. For example, in the Kochi region—facing the Pacific, in the southern part of Shikoku—we shift from 7.7 percent of carriers of the virus at 20 kilometers west of the city, to .65 percent at the eastern gates; from 5.6 percent at 45 kilometers east of the city on the coast to zero percent at 20 kilometers northwest of the city. In a radius of some 50 kilometers, the distribution of the HTLV-carrying populations seems to be extremely dispersed, and this endemic mixture owes nothing to the natural geo-climatic conditions particular to each of these micro-regions.

To what significations then could we refer this kaleidoscope? To the history of HTLV in Japan. And what this parceling-out indicates is that this history is *recent*. The biological history of HTLV in Japan is necessarily new, the virus was introduced into the country's history not long since, for if it were otherwise, the virus would have

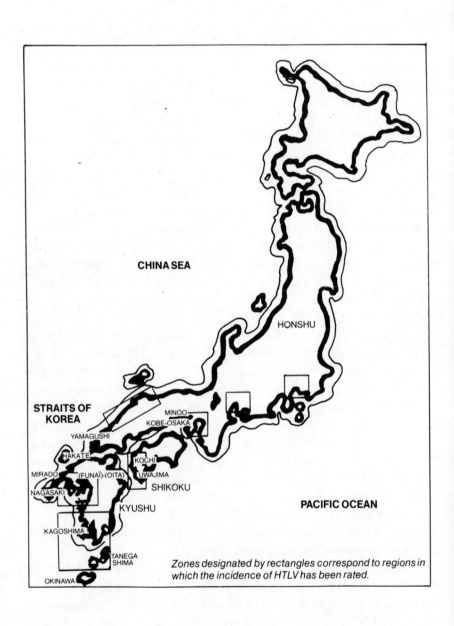

CHINA SEA

HONSHU

STRAITS OF
KOREA

MINOO
KOBE-OSAKA

YAMAGUSHI

HAKATE

KOCHI

MIRADO

UWAJIMA

(FUNAÏ)-(OITA)

SHIKOKU

NAGASAKI

KYUSHU

PACIFIC OCEAN

KAGOSHIMA

TANEGA
SHIMA

OKINAWA

Zones designated by rectangles correspond to regions in which the incidence of HTLV has been rated.

infallibly multiplied in a much greater number of individuals, in more widespread regions.

Thus, by contrast with the humans, the macaques of Japan, living wild in many regions of the southern and southwestern parts of the country, are carriers of various viruses, one of which seems to be a relative of human HTLV. Still, contrary to man, simian virus-carrying does not give rise to these phenomena of focalization. The study has just been made and concerns a total of 703 monkeys of different species. Of them, 302 have been recently captured in Japan in ten different rural localities, the rest in Taiwan and in the People's Republic of China, in India, and in Indonesia. Independent of their sites of capture—in Japan or elsewhere—the monkeys of the sensitive species of the Old World* are very often carriers of the virus related to HTLV. The percentage increases with the length of life and, on an average, 70 percent of the 10-year-old monkeys *(Macaca fusata)* are "positive." The "portage" density varies, of course, from point to point (10 percent at Miyajima, 95 percent at Minoo, northeast of Osaka), but no virgin zone has been found. Such a dissemination, whatever the monkey's volubility, requires time, and on the scale of Japan, centuries or tens of centuries. Hence it is likely that the monkey populations have known great intermixtures in the course of history and the polygamous activism of the males of simian society permits calculating a step-by-step sexual contamination in the course of time.

Humans, on the other hand, seem very reserved on this point, and sedentary. In the Kochi region, in fact, networks of communication and authorizations of displacement were, down to the end of the nineteenth century, *nonexistent.*

If the implantation of the human leukemic virus is recent, how recent is it? According to medical reports, the cutaneous disease that is the mark of the virus (Sezary's disease) was already noted on

---

*The "Old World" includes notably Africa and Asia, source of Homo sapiens humanity, in opposition to the New World (the Americas) where, anthropology teaches us, human beings appeared and developed later in the planet's evolution. The investigation has also included South American monkeys: all (35) tested negative for the simian HTLV virus.

Kyushu before the last world war. The Japanese ports of Nagasaki, Kagoshima, Kobe-Osaka, even if they might have constituted military bases for expeditions to the Pacific islands, Indonesia, and the Sunda Islands, would already have been "contaminated" by HTLV long before the attack on Pearl Harbor. Earlier, tracing back through history, Japan had reopened her harbors to the world at the end of the nineteenth century and Shanghai lies opposite Kyushu and its harbors Nagasaki and Kagoshima on the Eastern China Sea. However, recently conducted investigations among the Chinese populations of Shanghai province have shown only an exceptional incidence of the HTLV virus. The recent history of modern Japan therefore does not furnish us with a valid explanation for the concentration of carrier subjects in this part of the country. Tracing back still further, on the other hand, a curious pattern appears. Whether a fanciful coincidence or a truly significant one, HTLV's topographical distribution in the southwest of Japan is virtually a tracing of the local settlement of the Portuguese at the end of the fifteenth and the beginning of the sixteenth centuries.

In 1543, the first Portuguese sailors, pilots, and adventurers land in Japan on the little island of Tanegashima, south of Kyushu. In 1549, (Saint) Francis Xavier, an evangelizing proselyte, lands at Kagoshima. Upon his departure, several years later, he leaves missions, schools, churches, notably in the regions of Yamagushi (Honshu) and of Funaï-Oita, on the island of Kyushu, less than 100 kilometers by inland sea from Uwajima—zone of the HTLV endemy. The Western religion spreads. The merchants, initially Portuguese, then of all nationalities (Dutch, British, Spanish above all), benefit from the fact. The ports of Hirado and Hakate, on the northern side of Kyusho, were opened to them. The Spanish and Portuguese Jesuits were not far behind, neither in churches nor in markets. The Society of Jesus played its part in business and received Nagasaki in exclusive concession. For a while it was Jesuits who monopolized all trade, notably the lucrative market for raw silk. But the Christians were gradually expelled after 1614 or exterminated in the course of the century. In 1635 the Shogun's government forbade, on pain of death, all contacts between Japanese and occidentals, and Christianity was judged incompatible with domestic order because it was too closely linked to the alien powers. From exclusion to murder, the Portuguese lost their privileged positions to the advantage of the Dutch, closer to the necessities of this world than of the next, who managed to retain very closely supervised relations with the Japanese territories through the single officially open port of Nagasaki.

How can we connect and comprehend this surprising superposition of epidemiological (HTLV) and historico-geographical strata? Its signification may depend on Africa. Dutch and Portuguese had fought each other on the west coasts of central Africa, notably in Angola, at the gates of what is now Zaire, even before fighting each other in Japan. Now, HTLV is an "African" virus.

The data on Africa, and on the Africans living or having lived in Africa, is recent and still fragmentary. Nonetheless the first soundings within the black populations of Zaire indicate that the virus is present there. Further, a strain of HTLV virus recently has been developed from the lymphocytes of a native of this country. Collected in Paris in 1982, his cells had been transported to the United States in frozen ampoules. This strain will have been the first strictly African isolate of HTLV. The record of the HTLV situation in Africa overlaps the information coming from the New World. Here, the African origin of the virus appears without much ambiguity. In the United States and in Europe, the virus is extremely rare among whites, whereas it is "non-exceptional" (more than 1 percent) in the black populations of rural regions of the southwest United States. The first "American" strain of the virus had been obtained from the lymphocyte culture of a black man living in Alabama.

In the Caribbean, geographic "distribution" of the virus-carrying healthy populations matches an ethnological dispersal. Haiti is a known endemic zone; not Santo Domingo. The first black republic in the history of the New World at the beginning of the nineteenth century, Haiti welcomed rebels of African origin from the island of Hispaniola. The latter abandoned the Dominican "part" of the island, today still "white."

Martinique, Guadeloupe, Désirade are also regions of endemic HTLV, but not St. Barthélemy. All these islands are linked to French colonial history. Désirade is a few anchorages away from the very French free port of St. Barthélemy. Désirade, as will have been foreseen, has a black or mixed population, while that of St. Barthélemy is white: 3.5 percent of the Désiderais are healthy carriers of the virus. None of the St. Barthélemais tested is "positive." In Jamaica, Tobago, Panama, Surinam, the same overlap has been noted: the carrier population is decidedly of African lineage. There can be no doubt: HTLV's origin is in Africa. In Africa, where the slave traders landed, coming from Portugal, from Holland, from France, from England, from Spain, from the Arab countries.

Let us analyze the case of Haiti. The island was discovered in 1492 by Christopher Columbus's sailors. Haiti was then populated by a million natives, anything but hostile, judging from the explosive effects when the Spanish crew returned to their natal country. An extraordinary epidemic of syphilis broke over the world, ultimately reaching as far as the city of Canton, in China, in 1498. There were a million Haitians in 1492; they numbered less than 4,000 in 1535. Scarlet fever, measles, smallpox, yellow fever, and other Spanish-borne microbes will have transformed these lost pagans into 996,000 Christians saved for eternity. In 1502 Dr. Las Casas, a missionary priest in Haiti, seized with compassion for the Indians decimated there, suggested replacing the "missing" by blacks to be taken from the Guinea coast. HTLV's "natural"—*i.e.,* African—geography could have been remodeled by men in the maritime aftermath of the Renaissance. A heroic and certainly brutal period, when the captains of Palos and Noguères sailed off "to conquer the fabulous metal," as Heredia's poem has it, "which Cypango ripened in its distant mines," Cypango being Japan. Having sailed westward in search of a new passage to India and Japan, they discovered the Antilles. Colonial competition, reconciled according to an enormous "Yalta" at Tordesillas in 1494, confirmed the acquisitions and left Africa to Portugal. From the Cape Verde Islands they profitably controlled the gold route deflected from its trans-Saharan "Arab" path, and from there the

Portuguese reached the mouth of the Congo and Angola in 1482. Good sailors and famous pilots, they managed to overcome all obstacles, winds and contrary currents, opposing their southward descent into Africa. In 1497, Vasco da Gama, after Bartholomeu Dias, rounded the cape, with good hope of rivaling the Arabs and the Genoans in their spice trade with India, Asia, and eventually, Japan.

HTLV is an Old-World virus, an African virus, but not specifically a virus of Africans. HTLV is merely a virus, and it is without distinction of color or race that it takes up residence in those who are favorable to it. White or black, it matters not at all to the virus, and one of the very first isolates of the virus was obtained from the lymphocytes of a British sailor who had frequently visited Haiti.

The map of HTLV in the New World is that of the *African Diaspora*. But here, as in Japan, HTLV's distribution extends well beyond that of AIDS.* In Japan, the disease AIDS is rare. The virus HTLV, however, is widespread, an anomaly which we shall have to take into account when we draw up the prosecution for the HTLV-AIDS trial.

The dossier will be reinforced to the prosecution's advantage by a final indication: the modes of HTLV's propagation, studied by the Japanese epidemiologists, resemble those we were able to establish for the interhuman transmission of AIDS.

Contamination by HTLV

SEXUAL PROPAGATION

HTLV's transmission during intimate contact is asymmetrical: from man to woman, but less readily from woman to man.

Research has been conducted in Japan in regions where HTLV is

---

*The virus is frequent in certain Eskimo populations. The second victim in the history of HTLV is an American whose company was Aleutian. In his native village located in one of the southern Alaskan islands, the population is virus-carrying in a proportion of 1 out of 10. Coincidence? The Aleutian Islands were occupied from 1941 to 1943 by Japanese soldiers.

widespread among the population. Such investigation is retrospective where healthy carrier subjects (identified by anti-HTLV antibodies found in the carriers' blood) have served to trace epidemiological succession and to investigate families. When the "conductor" is a married man, the wife is in almost every case herself a carrier of the virus. Conversely, less than half the husbands of women virus-carriers are themselves carriers. These essential data have been corroborated by those obtained from simian HTLV from Japanese monkeys.

In the totality of the species of virus-carrying Japanese monkeys, the females are twice as numerous as the males. In order to document and understand these raw facts, a team of researchers from the Kochi region has undertaken the following experiment: young males, untouched by the virus, have been distributed one by one in cages containing a harem of contaminated females. The converse experiment consisted in placing a carrier male in contact with "virgin" females. At the end of the period of observation and mating, a blood sample was taken in order to establish the possible presence of anti-HTLV antibodies. Two conclusions appeared. First, the carrier males regularly transmit the virus to their female partners, while the carrier females are not so contagious, by a long shot (no male has been found contaminated). Secondly, the males are polygamous. This asymmetry of propagation is that of the AIDS virus. Follow the route of the cells and find the key to this asymmetry. The HTLV virus is a parasite on the cells; it multiplies only *in* a host cell. For HTLV, the latter is chiefly the T-lymphocyte, present in both monkey sperm and human sperm. The contaminated cells, "deposited" on a receptive mucous membrane, appear to be the vehicles of the virus's propagation. The receiver of the intimate secretions is therefore the only one susceptible to being contaminated.

THE HTLV VIRUS IS TRANSMITTED FROM MOTHER TO CHILD

The HTLV model-by-monkey shows that the progeniture of a carrier female is more often virus-positive (31 percent) than that of a non-carrier female (19 percent). Nonetheless, the male parents being not only promiscuous but also incestuous, it is difficult to establish precisely the mode of the virus's transmission.

In the offspring of carrier Japanese women, the incidence of carrier children increases with age. This "vertical" transmission from mother to child might occur during pregnancy or childbirth, through the placenta or by breast-feeding, since the mother's milk is rich in lymphocytes. But the trans-placentary means remains the only one documented to this day by the following observation: a young woman working in one of the research centers for HTLV was known as a healthy carrier of the virus. During her pregnancy, she was carefully followed and at childbirth a certain number of her research-colleagues were on the spot with flowers and a few pipettes, in order to take blood from the umbilical cord, a painless and harmless enterprise. The child's cells, perfectly developed, were put in culture and the HTLV virus isolated in the laboratory. Thus, contamination of the child must have occurred during pregnancy or childbirth, at that moment when the mother's blood is naturally transfused to the child through the placenta and the umbilical cord.

THE HTLV VIRUS IS TRANSMITTED BY MEANS OF BLOOD CELLS

In Japan, where incidence of the virus is relatively high among blood donors, in endemic regions of the southwest, it has been, retrospectively, possible to follow the virus from donor to receiver. Transfused fractions containing blood cells are associated with a rate of contamination higher than 60 percent. More than half the receivers become carriers of the virus in their turn.

T4-lymphophiliac, hemosexual, and exotic, HTLV is "leukemic," but we had the example of feline leukemia-AIDS virus. HTLV *or one of its close neighbors* conforms to the typical description of the AIDS virus.

The Alibis Collapse

A SCATTERED HTLV FOR A LIMITED AIDS?

Medico-detective investigation allowed us to establish the distinctive elements and signs of the AIDS virus, rediscovered word for word, or word against word (leukemia-aplasia) in the HTLV file; among the latter, geographical data occupied a strategic position. Considering these more closely, the number of healthy HTLV carriers on Kyushu contrasts with the absolute rarity—at least in appearance—of AIDS in this region of the world. Comparing Haiti and Kyushu on this point, endemic HTLV is two or three times weaker in Haiti, whereas AIDS there is two or three hundred times more frequent! An oddity approaching incoherence, to the point where we might be tempted to abandon our sleuthing.

Of course, the AIDS inquiries in Japan are not completed, and they are similarly under way in the Caribbean and in South America. Surinam, Mexico, Uruguay, and Brazil reported their first cases only at the end of 1983. But the difference between Haiti and Kyushu-Shikoku remains striking. Have the Japanese, since the time of the "initial" HTLV inoculation at the beginning of the sixteenth century become genetically "resistant" to the AIDS form of the HTLV virus, whereas subjects of African ancestry in the Antilles remained sensitive to it? An unthinkable explanation, in genetic terms. It would have seemed legitimate, therefore, either to exclude the HTLV hypothesis in AIDS altogether, or else to assume the existence of different types of HTLV.

Let us consider first of all, following the devil's advocacy, what the abandonment of the HTLV trail would "cost" us in facts and lost hypotheses.

• A T4-trope virus, transmitted by blood cells and sperm, present in the Caribbean, in equatorial Africa and in Kyushu, yet which would not be HTLV? Strange. For there is indeed in Japan at least one case of authenticated AIDS: that sedentary married woman whose lymphocytes carry the HTLV virus and the serum of anti-HTLV antibodies.

• Monsieur D., long after having received a transfusion of Caribbean blood, died of AIDS in Paris. Lymphocytes taken from him have produced a virus closely resembling a classic HTLV. Is this an accident?

• From 5 to 8 percent of the American homosexuals who have contracted AIDS and from 2 to 4 percent of the cases of French AIDS have developed certain antibodies against HTLV. Yet less than 1 percent of metropolitan French persons and scarcely 1 percent of the homosexual partners—AIDS "contacts" in the United States—have such antibodies in their blood. Is this an accident?

• Finally, from 50 to 80 percent of the subjects who have contracted AIDS, in Boston and in Paris, carry other antibodies associated with infection by the classic HTLV virus.*

An accident? Impossible!

Such coincidences were too tangible to be any such thing. They and geographical distribution simply oblige us to arrive at the following deduction: the HTLV virus in the healthy carriers and in the leukemic victims is *not exactly* the same as the AIDS-HTLV. The AIDS-HTLV would have kept a common share of its parent, recognizable by certain antibodies present in 50 to 80 percent of the sufferers. Was the geographical model of HTLV too broad in comparison to the centers of AIDS infection, so rarely Japanese? A revision was necessary, and offered us a major deductive hypothesis: AIDS-HTLV is a *cousin* of the classic HTLV virus, rare in Japan, more frequent in Africa and, today, in Haiti.

AIDS NOW AND HTLV PERMANENTLY?

HTLV is excused—an African virus, as old as the Old World. The AIDS epidemic is, without any possible evasion, recent, at least in the New World. Sporadic, the "first" cases date back, for the most

---

*These antibodies are discerned by the link they form with a segment of the virus present on the surface of cells deliberately infected by "classic" HTLV and which are put in contact with the victims' serum *in vitro*.

part*, only to 1976 or 1977, and all concern Europeans who had lived in tropical Africa. In North America, the beginning of the epidemic can be dated 1979–1980. Why had not the classic HTLV, which had been widespread since the sixteenth century, given rise to the exotic disease AIDS before 1979? Why weren't Europeans and Americans vacationing in the Caribbean before 1979 affected and contaminated? Of course, heterosexual men are less exposed to sexual contamination than homosexuals. But in Haiti, as we know, the majority of male cases are *not* homosexuals. Then HTLV? An ancestral virus for a "new" disease?

The defense seemed to score a point: the historical alibi seemed a likely one. And the bad faith of the prosecution was heard to murmur: Are we so sure of the newness of the disease in Haiti? Can we really know what was happening medically in the days of Papa Doc and his Tontons, the days of the worst black poverty? Yet the prosecution has just discovered in Japan that there are several members of the HTLV family, closely resembling one another but nonetheless distinct. The alibi was merely a hoax of *virus Amphitryons.*† Three new testimonies would permit us to arrive at a new conclusion: the HTLV-AIDS virus has recently appeared in Haiti.

HAITIAN DOCTORS ON THE STAND   By decree of (Western) arrogance, the dating of the disease in Haiti cannot rest on the testimonies of Third World doctors. It is true that the diagnosis of AIDS is not simple, technologically. It is also possible that the level of medical education is, as some may have experienced in our own regions, unevenly transmissible. We have citations, for example, of the *nonexistence* of Kaposi's sarcoma in Haiti until 1980 and then the sudden appearance of the skin disease in six months—six months which follow the installation in Port-au-Prince of a dermatologist of reliable training. But excluding such inferences, this would not prove

---

*An observation dated 1959 discovered in the medical archives describes a disease of AIDS type in a man who had traveled in tropical regions.

†The classic HTLV (leukemia) of Japan and the Caribbeans has been since designated HTLV-I. The newly discovered HTLV (AIDS) is being called HTLV-III. The initials H.T.L.V. in both types of viruses now stand for Human T-Cell Lymphotropic Virus.

that there were cases of Kaposi's in Haiti *before* 1980. And 1980 is the beginning of what will be, in 1983, an epidemic of AIDS. Finally and above all, most of the physicians who today see and recognize these victims in Haiti were already functioning there before 1980. The same physicians who, by their own souls and memories, swear that they had not previously seen such cases.

TOURISTS INTERROGATED The disease has "exploded" in the island's tourist centers, essentially in two neighborhoods of Port-au-Prince. No case, or virtually none, in the countryside, where the classic HTLV endemic is at least as consistent as in the cities. Intimate contacts between visitors and native populations, of whatever sex, do not date from yesterday. A number of Frenchmen had been quite happy in Haiti, without bringing home any nasty souvenirs. No AIDS at Club Med. or none, at least, until very recently.

TESTIMONY Hemophiliacs form a highly medicalized population in North America, considering their repeated transfusions of coagulant factor VIII of plasmatic origin. "Concentrates" of these fractions were widely used in the United States from the beginning of the seventies, concentrates which represent the coagulant quintessence of from 2,000 to 20,000 donors, plasmas mixed. Hemophiliacs have contracted AIDS in various countries of the world following such tranfusions. Now, the physicians and centers specializing in the treatment of hemophiliacs are categorical: after examining their files in every possible manner, including accounts of autopsies, they do not discover any recorded trace of AIDS *before* 1980. If the incubation delay after transfusion, the time separating the inoculation of the AIDS virus from the appearance of the first symptoms, is on an average of two or three years, we can consider that the shipments of coagulant fractions contaminated by the AIDS virus are *posterior* to 1976. Before 1976, the fractions used were, on the other hand, healthy.

What relation does all this have with the dating of AIDS in Haiti? The blood used in North America, before 1975, came largely from Latin America and the Caribbean, notably from Haiti. Since the beginning of the seventies, the blood industries used donors whom they could pay cheaply. The purchasers did not lack a certain sense of opportunity: in 1973, the Nicaragua earthquake claimed many victims and drew the sympathy, as well as the material and physical aid, of many volunteers from all parts of the Western world. Temporary camps were installed in modern, comfortable tents. In one of these, a huge one at that, a company producing the machine to "milk" plasma* installed its devices by the dozen. It was to gather a huge collection of plasma for commercial use at a rate of several hundreds of liters per week. Elsewhere, we recall the rumors of scandals provoked, from 1970 to 1972, by the traffic in blood from Haiti.† Bad blood, evidently, as some will have concluded, glancing at Haitian blood at the moment of AIDS. And yet, the thing is unlikely. After 1973 Haitian blood was no longer legally imported to the United States. Since the technology of massive plasmaphereses was now widespread, America would no longer have to depend on that particular blood source. After 1975, the Federal Food and Drug Administration would no longer grant its seal of approval to Haitian blood, nor to that of the majority of its former South American suppliers. Conclusion: the Haitian donor-sellers were not carriers of the AIDS virus before 1976, even if they were, no doubt, carriers of the classic HTLV-I virus in a proportion somewhere between 1 and 3 percent.

Who then imported or exported the AIDS virus, a member of the HTLV family, into Haiti after 1976 and still later? The medical pertinence of this question is no longer so clear as the preceding ones, and in order to implicate the HTLV family in the AIDS case, the prosecution does not need to answer on this point. The dossier shifts to the geopoliticians.

---

*The technique of massive plasmaphereses, or plasmatic exchanges, consists in "plugging" the donor's veins into a circuit which, by means of various processes, permits separating the plasma from the globules, and preserving only the former.

†The famous Hemo-Caribbean and Co. was financed from New York and supported by President Duvalier's brother-in-law.

The African Strain

History, ethnology, investigations into the HTLV endemic in the Caribbean—everything suggests that the leukemia brand of HTLV virus has long been present in Africa. On the other hand, the disease due to the AIDS virus has, in Zaire, an historical and clinical "marker": the serious and widespread form of disseminated Kaposi's sarcoma. But this disease was rare and not very contagious. Thousands of Europeans, and tens of thousands of Belgians, have lived in Zaire until the beginning of the 1960's and few (even none) have contracted a disseminated Kaposi's syndrome. The same is true for the French of Congo-Brazzaville. In the ecological and medicinal conditions (needles and syringes) of 1950–1975, the absence of diseases of epidemic proportions that can be linked to AIDS marks the history of these countries. Let us also note that the insects of the region, though carriers of malaria,* did little to disseminate the AIDS virus at the time. Reckoning from the middle 1970's, European cases of diseases, retrospectively assimilable to AIDS, are noted in Paris, in Brussels, in Copenhagen. "Epidemics" of serious "cryptocosis"† are reported in 1982. The Zaire emigration and the quite recent reports from Kinshasa testify to the numerical expansion of cases presently registered. Curiously, the historical articulation occurs, in Africa as in the Caribbean, around 1975. But what has happened in Africa? A question for geopoliticians, here again. Before we listen to what they have to say, it is of some interest to remark that other tropical viruses (without relation to AIDS) have on occasion undergone such spectacular promotions and that "new" diseases have unexpectedly appeared where there had been "nothing," epidemic versions of previously sporadic diseases in forgotten corners of the equatorial world. Models for an AIDS virus hitherto (1975–1976) hidden somewhere in the jungles of Zaire?

---

*The serious Kaposi's syndrome cases in Zaire are reported mainly in the humid zone, where mosquitoes carry the malaria agent.

†Due to a microbe responsible for an infection characteristic of AIDS.

HISTORY OF THE FEVERS OF MARBURG, OF LASSA, AND OF EBOLA

Marburg, West Germany, 1967: technicians in two laboratories of viral biology are one after the other affected by a violent fever with prostration and profuse bleeding. Twenty-five of them will be affected within three weeks, and seven will die. A virus hitherto little known, even unknown, will be isolated, and the source of the epidemic will be assigned to specimens, tissues, and cells from African monkeys brought to the laboratories from Kenya.

Lassa in Nigeria, 1969: a missionary sister of North American origin and a friend of hers, also a nun, die from an unexplained acute febrile disease. The friend had remained at her bedside, before falling ill in her turn. A third sister, nursing the first two, would be evacuated by plane to New York, having contracted a high fever, and would be cured of her unknown disease. But two laboratory technicians in Manhattan, who had examined the convalescent woman's blood, were themselves to fall ill. And one of the two succumbed.

Nzara, in the depths of Sudan, near the Zaire and Uganda borders, 1976: in a cotton-finishing factory appear several cases of hemorrhagic fevers unknown to the European doctors on duty there. In a few weeks, the disease affects a growing number of inhabitants in the nearby community. Two patients are evacuated to Maridi, 150 kilometers to the east, where there is a better medical facility—a large hospital with 230 doctors, orderlies, and technicians, 72 of whom will be affected in several weeks, and 42 of whom will die. All young trainees innocently dedicated to their new apostolate, all except for one doctor who had committed the sin as well as the imprudence of an intimate contact with one of the patients. The town of Maridi is infected in its turn and the volunteer investigators, sent from Cambridge, will note that the relatives of the first patients are the most frequently affected. The contamination seems to occur during the preparation of the dead for the funeral ceremonies. The corpses are subsequently burned or buried by the Western physicians themselves. And the epidemic dies out in Maridi. The "Ebola" fever will have claimed 284 victims, half of whom will die.

Zaire is 800 kilometers south of Maridi, linked to Sudan by a trail. A little mission hospital takes in one survivor of the Sudanese inferno, who recovers here from his disease. But 10 days after his stay, two or three weeks after the Maridi infection, the hemorraghic fever breaks out in and around the mission. One by one, 58 nearby villages are affected, 318 persons catch the disease, and more than 250 die. It is thought that one of the syringes or needles that had been used for the care of the Sudanese "contact" might have been reused for other patients. One of the nurses on duty in the mission hospital falls ill and is transferred to Kinshasa. Result: two dead at the Kinshasa hospital.

Three viruses, Marburg, Lassa, Ebola, and three "new" diseases had therefore been "discovered." The three probably derived from natural "reservoirs," animal reservoirs of viruses, perhaps from monkeys living in the jungle, and probably transferred to man by the intermediary of vector insects. Between the south-Sudan and the north-Zaire mission, a trail blazed through the equatorial jungle, where there is no lack of insects and where animals, potential reservoirs of incredible viruses, abound. The tropical forest is opened, but its buried treasures are of various kinds.

Geopolitics of AIDS

The HTLV-AIDS strain, if it had always been present in the tropical regions where the "new" disease today breaks out, must have been rare there, initially a few sporadic cases at most. Two factual pegs enable us to verify this interpretation:

1. No hemophiliac in the United States had contracted AIDS before 1980, whereas the blood used to produce the coagulant fractions came in part from Haiti, a zone of classic HTLV endemia from the time of the deportation of African slaves.
2. Europeans in Africa did not contract AIDS before 1975.

Where did the HTLV-AIDS strain come from, by what itinerary, and when would it have spread? Our three "takes" leave little time for exploration: 1974–1977. Is it thinkable that the strain could have spread simultaneously, but independently, in Haiti and in equatorial Africa? Is it thinkable that it could have transited from Haiti to Zaire, without an exit ticket in the population movements traceable in that direction during the period designated? By subtraction, there remains, the strictly African origin* of the present explosion, and the precedent of the hemorrhagic fevers of Marburg, Lassa, and Ebola provides us with a possible African scenario for AIDS.

Granted that disposable (but not discarded) plastic syringes reached Africa long after the first bottles of Coca-Cola. But would this suffice to spread the HTLV-AIDS strain over such great distances? Characterized as an amplification of a "natural" phenomenon, no doubt. But we also require a reservoir, an animal one for instance,† freed from its initially limited geography by local ecological modification. Who at this period could have "opened" the Zaire jungles or those of the neighboring countries and thereby spread the hidden virus in this fashion? Who might have exported it from there to the New World? Who in the recent history of human mobility might have followed such an itinerary? The Cubans, perhaps. After all, did they not physically intervene in Angola in 1972 and subsequently? We know, from the evidence of visual testimony, that there were many Cuban soldiers in the northern part of the country, not far from Zaire during 1977, in jungle regions. Carried by such veterans, the virus might have pursued its long journey in the direction of the United States. In 1977–1978, the Cuban government expelled a certain number of undesirables among whom figured *"magalitas"* (homosexuals) and Angola veterans. A certain number of the latter found refuge in Florida, in Miami. Miami and southeast Florida is a

---

*The serious form of Kaposi's syndrome was known in equatorial Africa for over 20 years. This extremely rare disease (at the time) seems to be having a notable expansion in Zaire today.

†The Kenya macaques *(Sarcopithes ethiops)*, whose blood, analyzed in West Germany, contains, in 95 out of 100 animals tested, simian anti-HTLV antibodies, belong to the species of monkeys in which the Marburg virus had been discovered.

recognized zone of "swinging" homosexual activity, a boat-trip from the island of heterosexual protectionism. Miami, a \$95 round-trip from Port-au-Prince, exotic turntable of the American and Caribbean worlds. Miami, fourth largest center of AIDS in the United States, just behind the three gay megalopolises. Miami, linked to them by long chains of homosexual fraternity of the type: Miami–Haiti, Los Angeles–Haiti, New York–Haiti–Miami. Thus might have been born a new epidemic, out of the jungle depths of Africa into the Western world.

Confrontations and Final Conclusions

Might there be other viruses to indict? Several candidates have come forward; others will suggest themselves in turn, so long as the formal indictment of HTLV has not been pronounced.

THE KENYAN VIRUS AND THE CUBAN PIGS: THE CIA THROUGH AIDS

An epidemic of deadly fevers ravaged the Cuban swine-stocks, beginning in 1975. At its source, an African strain of virus* whose first victims had been hogs from the Kenya plateaus, some years before. Kenya-Angola-Cuba-AIDS, such might have been the chain of importation,† either through contaminated animals or else, according to the testimony of a former member of the famous "agency," by the direct and malicious contamination of the Cuban hogs financed by the CIA. Despite its seductive exotico-historical features, however, this outsider virus is neither retro-, nor humanophiliac, nor T4-trope, nor present in Japan. Yet it briefly took the lead among the virus-candidates for AIDS, in the highly imaginative period of

---

*The virus of the Kenyan hogs belongs to the family of "parvo-viruses," germs of small size capable of provoking immune anomalies in young pigs or even defects of maturation of human blood cells. The swine virus does not infect humans.

†The coincidence of the epidemic of African swine fever in Cuba with that of AIDS in the New World remains nonetheless striking.

the first quarter of 1983. Now set aside by the results of soundings made in the blood of a certain number of victims: negative.

THE PASTEUR VIRUS

A team of virologists at the Pasteur Institute led by doctors Barre-Sinoussi Chermann, and Montagnier, had also followed the HTLV clue to AIDS, in the first quarter of 1982. Trained in the techniques of cell culture favorable to the growth of HTLV (one of them had visited Dr. Robert Gallo's laboratory at Bethesda in July 1982), they had been notified of the HTLV hypothesis by the material on AIDS sent out by the Groupe de Travail Français. Armed with these technical and conceptual elements, they were the first to discover in two victims a retrovirus close to the classic HTLV according to certain criteria, but different from it according to other characteristics. The initial designation of their retrovirus, Human T-cell *Lymphotropic* virus, differentiated the latter from the human T-cell *leukemia* virus, from Japan and from the Caribbean, while preserving the same initials HTLV. A year later, it would become clear that they had doubtless grown the first specimens of the AIDS brand of the leukemia HTLV, sought for as the AIDS malefactor and today designated HTLV-III/LAV (for Lymphadenopathy Associated Virus; lymphadenopathy = swollen lymph nodes, glands).

WHY WAS THE HTLV HYPOTHESIS BEST?

The procedure that led us to HTLV will have sought a gradual integration of facts into a totality while trying, at each step, not to add too many "gratuitous" hypotheses. The probability of their being on the wrong track will have increased with the quantity of uncertainty which their "gratuitousness" may have introduced.

What could link such disparate facts as a low number of T4-cells in the blood; T4-cells with perturbed functions; T4-cells razed, as seen in autopsy; transmission through the blood; Haiti; Africa; Japan; was the following series: a virus infects and affects the T4-cells and it is a tropical virus (HTLV). The leukemia-aplasia displacement made us run a risk, of wandering *or* of progress: T4-leukemia–T4-aplasia, a link of biological contraries that reinforces the totality by diminishing its cost, according to the figure of antinomy whose force of articulation formal logic teaches us.

T4-leukemia is, at least, *one* perturbation of the cellular machine linked to the *integration* of a retrovirus in the nucleus. A retrovirus also for AIDS but different either by its structure, or by its sites of cellular integrations or, more generally, its effects. The infected cell ages, is paralyzed or asphyxiated by the poisons the virus makes it secrete. Gratuitous hypotheses which no convincing fact has yet come to support. But they "cost" nothing, for they remain outside the main body of evidence. It remained to cross-check the geographic areas extending beyond the field of observation. HTLV-Japan: hardly any AIDS; HTLV-Haiti: AIDS = two different but related viruses with common structures. Each deductive stage permitted *inferring* the next. The final closing-in was "best" only because it integrated all the evidence into a coherent whole.

This method is not a new one. We find it recommended in the logic manuals of the sciences. But it is new in relation to the conceptual instruments used by science of microbes at the end of the nineteenth century and well into the first half of the twentieth. The chief difficulties and efforts of the discipline were turned not upon logic but rather technique. To be able to cultivate a virus *in vitro*, a bacterium starting from a piece of tissue or another biological specimen—such was its problem. Today, the culture of cells has emerged from its early stages and the microbic problem is, first of all, that of a choice. Which among the microbes a cytoculture produces are we to consider as the one which counts for history? We know too well the artifices of cytoculture to take seriously the first virus, selected by the conditions of the culture itself, solely because it "grows." It must also resemble the one which the investigation has permitted delineating. In this delineation, each element, without hierarchy, contributes its bit of information: molecular, cellular, clinical, geographical, historical, sociological. HTLV, which united all this into one, had a great deal about it to seduce logic. At the lowest costs.

Finally a Pascalian and opportunist wager, that of medicine (seen this time from the viewpoint of the medical profitability of an hypothesis), the *interest* of the HTLV hypothesis was to be already operative for prevention, since we already knew of the modes of transmission of HTLV-I (leukemia) in Japan. The mass of knowledge on this well identified and characterized HTLV-I would allow us to gain time.

Thereupon, having reread the elements of the investigation, the arraignment will now read as follows: Considering that Human T-Lymphotropic viruses represent a retrovirus family infecting and affecting cells of the same type as those diseased from the AIDS virus; that HTLVs are tropical viruses one strain of which (HTLV-I) has long been rampant in Africa in areas which recently have been a focus for AIDS; that traces of the passage of a member of the HTLVs are detectable in the serum of a growing number of victims (who have no ethnic or geographic reasons to carry such an "exotic" virus); that there are no other serious candidates that would so well fit the role of the AIDS-agent, we thereby declare that the responsibility for AIDS is incumbent upon HTLVs and their family. Let us speed up with the trial and hastily proceed to the only important tasks of neutralizing and eradicating them.

These conclusions were given to the publisher in Paris on January 31, 1984. Positive testimony from France and America revealing the presence of AIDS HTLV in at least 90 percent of the patients was known to everyone by May 1984.

The history of AIDS is that of an exotic virus newly introduced into the Western world. Its progress is now quite clear. The AIDS virus made its appearance in Haiti, starting in the mid-seventies. A small number of carriers of the virus somehow reached Port-au-Prince. Sexual contacts would multiply the occasions of the virus's passage. But women constituted an impasse, or a semi-impasse, to propagation. On the other hand, contamination of men by other men via contaminated secretions assured the transmission of the infectious agent. By homosexuals much more than by women. But, Officer, why homosexuals? Because they make love with each other! And in this creation, homosexual men have an ambivalence of pseudo-hermaphroditic type for the majority among them. A duality favorable to the passage of a virus from a "receiver" subject who becomes a "donor" in his turn. The relative intransitivity of hetero-sexual propagation would simply abide by this biological fact, which puts women in position to "receive" intimate secretions and less, according to the primary logic of natural anatomy, in a "donor" position. The chains of homosexual contacts with multiple partners has on the evidence helped to amplify this means of human contami-nation, receiving and giving their sperm to other men.

For biology, the moral of the story might be: viruses are where they happen to be. It suffices to go looking for them, to encounter them in such places, in order to be infected by them. AIDS is a tropical disease, brought back by men from their "exotic" journeys.

·*Part Two*·

THE AIDS-EFFECT

· 1 ·

HAITI: INFAMY AND PREJUDICE

DURING THE FIRST HALF OF 1982, THE NATIONAL CENTERS FOR disease control in Atlanta registered 34 AIDS cases among Haitians of both sexes who had recently emigrated to the United States. On the island itself, a certain confusion prevailed: the "reality" of AIDS was not acknowledged, though a report on Kaposi's disease concerning Haitians had been presented at a colloquium held in Port-au-Prince in May 1982. The disease was nonetheless "discovered" here by Western agents working for the Epidemiology Intelligence Service, a branch of the National Institutes of Health in Bethesda, Maryland. Installed on the island under various labels, the EIS agents discreetly noted several dozen cases during 1982–1983. Outside the island, several dozen Haitian refugees—in Paris, in Montreal, in Quebec, and in French Guiana—were acknowledged to have contracted AIDS, starting in 1982. Today the Haitian doctors have officially registered over 150 cases on the island, all in Port-au-Prince and Carrefour, centers for American and European tourists. In January 1984 at least 300 cases of the disease could be counted, *intra-* and *extra-muros.*

With a few nuances of its own, AIDS in Haiti can be superimposed on the observed form of the disease elsewhere. However, the mode of contamination by the viral agent remains uncertain for a considerable percentage of the cases. Homosexual transmission represents only a fraction of the total and, outside of a few intravenous drug users and three post-transfusional cases, most have occurred in an entirely unexplained manner among heterosexual men and women. The proportion of men to women affected is about equal, subtracting the cases of male homosexuals. The transcutaneous mode remains, here as in Africa, a possibility. Itinerant inoculators are on the scene. Disposable plastic injection materials, improperly reused, might play their part in the spread of the *newly* introduced virus. But, as postulated, heterosexual transmission is also, as it is in Africa, most likely.

The disease did not exist in Haiti before 1975, and it must have been imported from central Africa, directly or indirectly. Subjects—of either sex—of North American and European origin have contracted the disease in Haiti, after transfusion or under circumstances not yet fully elucidated (sexual contacts with persons carrying the HTLV-III agent?).

The Stigma of the Risk Group

The disease and its causative virus appeared on the island a few years ago. For Americans, one of the essential immediate problems was to circumscribe the population groups susceptible of being carriers of the agent in order to stray them aside from blood collection. In 1983, there were no biological tests enabling this designation to be applied for certain. The teeth of the comb were wide apart at this time. Any person theoretically susceptible of being a carrier of the virus had to be, if possible, separated from the donors. It was then that the trade mark "risk group" or "group at risk" appeared, applied to the whole of the Haitian nation. The technical logic—to separate the blood donors—had a character at once unavoidable ("We don't know how to recognize dangerous blood types, hence we'll eliminate all Haitians") and intolerable. Haitians are easily "recognizable" by their features and their culture. They are French-speaking blacks. The procedure that imposed this designation was discriminatory. It singled out the Haitians as a geographic entity, whereas the figures of incidence were scarcely different in this population from that of New York City: 1.16 cases for every 10,000 in the New York population, compared to 1.66 cases for every 10,000 people in Haiti. Now we have seen no posters urging all New Yorkers to abstain from giving blood. In fact, the Haitian people as a whole, marked *hereditarily* by its ethno-cultural features, found itself, with regard to AIDS, in the same position as other sociocultural groups with sociologically *acquired* characteristics: homosexuals or intraveneous drug users. The crime of racial discrimination with regard to the entire Haitian nation was imminent. Especially since the Haitian label excluded non-national residents who had lived on the island and who logically should have been included in this conglomeration, as they are today.

The Impact

In the United States, Haitians were literally "targeted": poor, black, "contagious," illegal immigrants. Between the homosexuals and the drug addicts, opprobrium was at its height: employers fired; others refused to hire; landlords were unwilling to rent or else insisted on disinfecting the premises; the intercepted boat people were impounded in camps or special jails; legal immigrants were locked up in ghettos. Non-Haitian populations living close by experienced an understandable terror: foreigners carrying a mortal germ that was said to be extremely contagious!

In Haiti the repercussions assumed a catastrophic dimension. The victims who raise—here as elsewhere—unsolved therapeutic problems were relatively numerous in relation to the country's sanitary and technical capacities. Economic pressure also made itself felt: tourist trade, a primary source of income, collapsed. After having so vociferously denied *everything*, the Haitian authorities now sought to confront their difficulties by attacking the homosexuals. They decided that "Haiti, under the direction of its president Jean-Claude Duvalier, would not become the brothel of the Caribbean." Faithful to its authoritarian traditions, the government closed certain hotels; certain foreigners were expelled and certain natives jailed. In July 1983, 70 of these were arrested at Port-au-Prince by the state police. This wave of arrests was interrupted when, according to a Haitian newspaper published in Brooklyn, the police were obliged to question, for the same reason, certain official personalities involved in the government, including the minister of foreign affairs.

The gravity of the situation, local and international, mobilized Haitians of every description: opposition, emigrant, or officials on the island. All were affected by the image of the Haitian people thus hawked abroad. The Haitian lobby in New York State was powerful; it galvanized into action on the question of AIDS and made its pitch to the political and health authorities. American representatives were solicited. The Haitians' electoral power was far from negligible, based on a rather conservative group of immigrants. The Haitian government reacted, delegating its representatives to international organizations. Sufficiently to obtain a reorganization of the facts and a less discriminatory formulation. In this spirit, the ambassador in Washington set a precedent in the history of Western medicine: a written intervention in the *New England Journal of Medicine*, in which he deplored the damage done by North American semantic carelessness to commerce and business.

Today, the facts are better established and the consensus accepted. The description "Haitians = risk group" has been withdrawn from the official documents of the World Health Organization. The disease and all its problems remain. These difficulties are shared by other underdeveloped countries facing the AIDS "explosion." Zaire, in its turn, is in the line of fire. Will this African nation be treated as "savagely" as Haiti was?

THE BLOOD PUZZLE

THE AIDS VIRUS IS TRANSMITTED BY BLOOD AND ITS DERIVATIVES. The contaminating donors are either diseased or healthy carriers of the virus.

Which Blood Products Are Involved?

Three types of blood products are involved in the transmission of the disease: whole blood (plasma plus corpuscles), blood corpuscles separated from the plasma, and the clotting fractions for hemophiliac use.

Whole blood is used chiefly in open-heart surgery or emergency surgery. In open-heart surgery, blood circulation is artificially maintained by a pumping system and an extra-corporeal circuit "primed" by blood. Emergency surgery for hemorrhaging wounds uses whole blood to compensate for losses sustained by the victim. This was the case with Monsieur D., the Haitian executive who had to receive an emergency transfusion of several units of fresh blood collected from Haitian donors, at least one of whom was a carrier of the AIDS virus.

"Concentrates" of blood corpuscles (most of the plasma is eliminated) serve to compensate for anemias in which either red corpuscles are missing or white corpuscles or platelets (small corpuscles active in the natural phenomena of clotting). Platelet concentrates were responsible for AIDS in one North American baby. *In toto*, more than one hundred cases of post-transfusion AIDS have been counted, almost all in the United States. These cases grow more numerous, month by month.

Anti-Hemophiliac Fractions

Until the fall of 1984 Europe had no case of AIDS following blood transfusion for surgery or some illnesses. However, some hemophiliacs from France, Spain, Great Britain, Switzerland, and Austria (and probably now from other European countries) have contracted AIDS. In the USA, AIDS cases among hemophiliacs already represent some 3.6 patients per thousand (October 1984).

All the world around many hemophiliacs, when they become treated for their congenital coagulation disorder, will receive blood or its derivatives in quantities that vary according to individual needs and to medical tactics chosen to protect them from bleeding. Accordingly, they will receive concentrates of red cells or of all blood. But above all, in order to compensate for their hereditary lack of clotting factor, they are prescribed perfusions of blood fractions enriched with factor VIII, known as anti-hemophiliac factor. Four sources of factor VIII–enriched fractions are available to them: simple cryo-precipitate (from a single donor); lyophilized cryo-precipitates which regroup the blood of several donors; intermediate concentrates from a dozen donors; and "super-concentrates" obtained from the blood of several thousand donors. These super-concentrates are prepared industrially and distributed on an international scale. The other three types of coagulant fractions are produced by local or national blood banks.

A given hemophiliac receives in his lifetime various types of blood fractions according to circumstances. Hence it has been difficult to discover, in a hemophiliac who has developed AIDS, *the* blood product which might have been the source of the contamination.

The total statistical data on the AIDS of hemophiliacs have furnished some indications on this point, but no certainties. In all the cases for which the investigation posssessed sufficient data, one common element has been found. All had received, at least once, "super-concentrates" whose chief characteristic resides in the astronomical number of different plasmas necessary to their fabrication, plasmas then mixed with each other: up to 20,000 different donors. It would suffice, theoretically at least, for a *single* carrier of the AIDS virus to be among them in order to contaminate the entire batch.

How Are the Anti-Hemophiliac Fractions Prepared?

The coagulant fractions are extracted from the plasma of non-hemophiliac donors. Plasma, the liquid part of the blood, is in principle separated from the blood cells. This separation is achieved during one or two centrifugations.* By the effect of centrifugal force, the cells, heavier and denser than the plasmatic liquid, fall to the bottom of the centrifuging flask and the "surfacing" plasma is collected. Now, if the AIDS virus is transmitted like its parent HTLV-I (leukemia), a study conducted in Japan in 1983 furnished us with a possible relevant model: *plasma alone does not transmit HTLV-I (leukemia)*.

No receiver of plasma from single donors carrying HTLV-I in their blood have in their turn become carriers of HTLV-I. On the contrary, 60 percent of those infused with whole blood or cellular components of blood from HTLV-I carriers have themselves become infected to the virus within three months following transfusion. At first, there would be a total incoherence between the indisputable transmission of the AIDS virus, HTLV-III/LAV, by certain factor VIII concentrates prepared from plasma and the (fortunate) failure

---

*An operation which consists in augmenting the gravity 1,000 to 5,000 times in a machine rotating at great speed.

to transmit HTLV-I with plasma alone. Thus HTLV-III/LAV would appear to behave differently from HLTV-I in this respect.

However, one cannot consider as plainly alike plasmas obtained from single donors and super-concentrates of factor VIII representing mixtures of plasma from thousands of donors. For instance, contaminating blood cells or cell fragments might not be in sufficient quantities in one given plasma, but more numerous in plasma concentrates. Accordingly, if it is true that plasma contains virtually no red or white blood corpuscles, some centrifuged plasma still contains a small number of platelets.* As a matter of fact, during the procedures of extraction and concentration of factor VIII some platelets have been found. Certain batches of factor VIII have up to 100,000 of them per microliter. The platelets could play the role of sponges, absorbing on their surface various substances, notably viruses. They also might be directly infected by the AIDS virus. Retroviruses not immediately related to the AIDS virus have been cultivated from platelets from certain patients. Another element of uncertainty: before being stockpiled, concentrates are sterilized by a process of microfiltration through extremely fine membranes the diameter of whose pores is in principle much smaller than that of a blood platelet. Contradictions persist, as we can see, between the epidemiological data, which seem to designate the super-concentrate fractions, though these are in principle free of blood-cell elements, and the non-transmission of HTLV-I in the absence of such blood-cell elements. If we retain the HTLV-I model for blood transmission of the AIDS virus, HTLV-III/LAV, it should be checked whether the concentrates still contain blood cells or filterable cell debris. However, it may just turn out that HTLV-I and III differ in respect to their capacity to survive or not survive in platelet-poor plasma.†

---

*Small corpuscles in blood participating in coagulation processes. Their density is so light that during centrifugation they will not "come down" as readily as the heavier red and white blood cells. Spinning platelets off plasma requires harsh conditions of centrifugation.

†One chimpanzee that was recently (1984) injected with plasma from a single patient with AIDS has developed symptoms compatible with an HTLV-III infection. Thus, plasma would seem to contain the AIDS virus under an infective form although we do not know to what extent the injected plasma was platelet-deprived.

What Is the Source of the Blood Used in the Production of Anti-Hemophiliac Fractions?

The concentrated fractions of factor VIII have been used for the last five years throughout the world by a growing number of hemophiliacs. They are produced industrially by five laboratories of worldwide scope: Armour, Behring, Cutter, Immuno, Travenol, in the United States as well as in Europe. They utilize the same methods of extraction and filtration while utilizing at least 90 percent of American commercial plasma.

What is the source of the blood collected? Most of it, it appears, comes from the United States. The industries concerned have local stations of massive plasmaphereses, collecting up to 50 liters of plasma a year from a single "donor." Of the six million liters thus collected, the United States "consumes" five and sells the sixth to European countries. Further, the United States buys on the European market some tens or hundreds of thousands of liters of plasma. "Mixtures" and "circuits" make investigation very difficult.

In order to discover the geographic origin of the plasmas, the precise inventory of the sources does not seem to be necessary. As a matter of fact, we know that blood from Latin America is not in question. Haiti, except for unlikely contraband, has sent no plasma to the United States in nearly 10 years. And the Nicaragua center, still accredited, it appears, collects in a region exempt from AIDS, as far as one knows. It is out of the question that the plasmas used in the United States could come from equatorial Africa. There remains, consequently, the American plasmas themselves. Plasma "donors," though they are paid a fixed amount of money, come from various sociological strata and behave according to different motivations. The homosexual community, in the mid-1970's, had been specifically called upon to contribute and solicited to participate in giving plasma to serve in the preparation of vaccine against hepatitis B. On the other hand, the money paid for these substances especially attracts those who, lacking other socially lucrative productions, can sell their plasma. Among these are drug addicts, without cash and in urgent need. Now, it is among the donors of these two populations that we are to expect to find those carrying the AIDS virus.

To Identify Contaminated Blood

"Transmission of AIDS through the blood and its derivatives." "AIDS is transmitted in the same way as hepatitis B." An understandable panic supervened in the United States blood centers. No one would venture into them any more, and the secretary of health would have to set a courageous example in a New York center where, publicly and unflinchingly, she gave her blood.

Compared to AIDS, hepatitis B is highly contagious. Its virus is transmitted through the blood and during intimate contacts, but also by all secretions, digestive as well as genital. Virus B, for instance, is present in the throat of its carriers. Further, during the manipulation of blood samples, the risk of contamination is considerable. Twenty percent of the medical—and paramedical—personnel are victims of a usually benign infection from hepatitis B during accidental punctures or contact with specimens from patients by the relay of minor wounds. The contagiousness of hepatitis B, as we see, does not have much to do with that of the AIDS virus. As of today, we can defuse the initial explosive model.

The AIDS Virus Is Not Transmitted Like the Hepatitis B Virus, But Rather Like HTLV-I

This nuance makes all the difference, since in the region of Kochi, in southwest Japan, endemic HTLV has remained localized and parceled out for generations within families carrying this virus.

A major problem is born with AIDS: the detection of carriers of the virus and the isolation of their blood, except for scientific purposes. A real puzzle for those in charge of blood banks, even if the risks of contamination by this means are evidently minimal for a subject receiving a transfusion.

The HTLV-variant hypothesis has been fully confirmed. It will give us, in the short run, the technical means of accounting for a majority of dangerous bloods by seeking antibodies against this type of virus in the donors. Other biological "markers" had been under study. None was specific to infection from the AIDS virus, and had they been adopted they would have led to eliminating blood of assuredly non-AIDS subjects. Those risk groups include: male homosexuals, especially those with many partners (more than 10 a year); intravenous users of hard drugs; men and women having resided or traveled during the last four years in one of the tropical regions where AIDS is today recognized: Haiti, equatorial Africa. In a certain number of Western countries, the application of this plan consists first of all of informing donors and asking them to identify themselves, in confidence, as belonging to one of these groups. Applied strictly, this system of exclusion will eliminate a number of blood donors who do not harbor the virus in their blood cells. It goes without saying that it is applicable only in non-tropical zones. For the Caribbean and Africa, the problem remains untouched, until we can profitably use the new techniques of screening for the AIDS variant of HTLV.

Anxiety as to Certain Products

AIDS in hemophiliacs has naturally led to questioning the harmlessness of other blood derivatives. The most obvious targets have been the vaccines against hepatitis B. Prepared with plasmas containing particles of virus B, they are theoretically susceptible of containing the AIDS virus. Plasma donors used for the preparation of the vaccine belong to the risk groups from which, precisely, voluntary exclusion from blood donation is being sought today because of the AIDS danger. An apparently circular, and insoluble, problem.

A vaccine against hepatitis, whatever the method of its production, is a remote derivative of plasma. The particles of virus B used in these vaccines are here in a free state, outside any cellular element. The anti-hemophiliac concentrates suspected of transmitting the AIDS virus do not benefit from the many stages of purification necessary to the preparation of the anti-hepatitis B vaccines. The latter contain little except for the vaccinating particles, and in no case do they contain residual cells. From this fact, we can ascertain that if it is true that HTLV-III/LAV has the same properties of transmission as those of HTLV-I, it is unthinkable that these vaccines can transmit the AIDS virus. Finally, to the stages of purification and inactivation are added one or several stages of chemical neutralization which should eliminate any residual infecting virus.

Against this technical and theoretical background, there had been since 1975 a commercial warfare between the two great world producers of vaccines, one American, the other French. Today, the World Health Organization has put an end to the struggle by acknowledging the validity of the modes of preparing the various vaccines offered to the public insofar as they "utilize *several* stages of inactivation."* Thereby, no case of AIDS transmission has been imputable to vaccination, in the United States or in France; nor to other plasma derivates such as albumin fractions or gamma globulin. Here, too, the absence of any cellular element in these products would render transmission of the AIDS virus theoretically impossible.

Beyond these controversies, AIDS has been the occasion of questioning anew the harmlessness of "other people's" blood. During recent years, medical literature has registered, virus after virus, the sources of infection which blood can represent. Blood, a natural product, thereby risks losing its "aura" in the long run. The practice

---

*Nonetheless the German health authorities continue to reject the French vaccines prepared from American plasmas. A decision regarded as arbitrary by the French industry, which has lodged an appeal with the competent authorities. Recent data (October 1984) have shown that HTLV-III/LAV was duly inactivated under the conditions that have been used for the French vacicine.

of auto-transfusion* will thereby have a lasting vogue, as will synthetic products replacing certain constituents (notably red corpuscles). To render blood harmless on the microbic terrain once again becomes a technological priority. The "mixtures" of blood coming from all corners of the world must be reduced, and the donor-sellers of blood in the Third World or the New World questioned once again. Ultimately, one can assume that medical indications resorting to the manna of blood will be defined in a stricter and hence more restrictive fashion.

---

*In countries where "other people's" blood is rare or when such blood is not acceptable (Jehovah's Witnesses), we can stockpile the subject's own blood in order to retransfuse him with it, if necessary, during or after an operation.

· 3 ·

AIDS, HOMOSEXUALITY, DOCTORS, SOCIETY

WHAT SUBJECTS FOR HISTORIANS, PHILOSOPHERS, SOCIOLOGISTS, AND preachers to write their books about! And no doubt these books are already written. Others will follow. AIDS will have had its letters patent of modernity.

A Modern Disease, or an Archaic Disease in a Modern World?

"Of or characteristic of the present time," says Webster of the word *modern*. AIDS is certainly that!

The disease sets in on a tide of "image-repertoires" affecting our lives as *Time* or, in Paris, *Actuel* reports them: sex and its liberalization, of which promiscuity is both the sign and the stigma. Sex and exoticism: Is not the tropical virus a strange fruit coming from "elsewhere"? Sex and travel: the great charter flights put Europe only a few hundred dollars away from New York. Sex and war: the rejects of Cuba, *magalitas* that blossomed in Angola—were they the ones who brought back the killer microbe to the New World? Sex and human misery: whereby the starving boat people from Haiti carried the disease to Miami. Sex and male prostitution: sexual activism on the grand scale, and all its resonance of insomniac frenzy, of promiscuous performance only a step away from sexual Stakhanovism and the obsessions of an anxious and overheated world.

Is there anything new for biology and for medicine in the history of AIDS? Granted, here biology applies its most recent knowledge: retroviruses and cellular cancerization. Certain medicaments already utilized, others for tomorrow, are and will be ultramodern. Alpha and gamma interferons derive from the most recent kinds of biological technologies, the DNA recombinants.* Medicine, confronting AIDS, faces a new epistemology, implicating the crossroads of every discipline capable of furnishing positive information.

But a virus is the most archaic biological entity there is: a product of the nucleic acid series as old as the world of the living. And medicine, once past the first astonishments of this new microbic affront—has it not seen its alike? Another once-modern disease, resembling AIDS in its tropical, sexual genesis and its importation into Europe from the (at the time very) New World, is in every handbook. It appeared at a detour on the road to western modernity: 1453, the fall of Constantinople. The Arabs, merchants and soldiers, control the overland trade routes to the Indies. To avoid the Islamic glacis by either the western or southern route is *the* project of the Western nations, which have acquired the means (cartography and the art of navigation) to sail the high seas. From the West Indies, discovered by the restless Columbus, comes a certain Treponema pallidum† that will have Europe paled with terror and, in less than five years, contaminate China.‡ Alternatively, a French or Neapoli-

---

*The alpha or gamma interferons are proteins. Their composition in amino acids follows an order corresponding, acid by acid, to a nucleic acid sequence within the chromosome. These sequences of genetic information have been isolated by means of enzymatic scissors whose tips are provided with special chemical signals , wrapped in molecular "vectors," the whole inserted within the genome of bacteria. These "recombinant" bacteria will express the new genic information and produce the human protein: "recombinant."

†Treponema pallidum is the agent of syphilis.

‡Despite the closing of the main route to the Indies, it would appear that the route of international sexuality had not been closed.

tan disease, depending on whether the Spanish mercenaries, its carriers and victims during the siege of Naples (1495), were on the side of Charles VIII or of Ferdinand II.

One epidemic resembles the next. The cases are always counted, the dead still listed: humans have an extraordinary sense of macabre administration. In Atlanta, 1983, the distribution of pentamidine, an antibiotic against pneumocystis, has doubled every six months since 1981. In Orvieto in 1489, the plague had made its black swaths through the population; the city-council ledgers noted the sizable increase of wax imports from the Levant—the wax from which funeral candles are made. Archaism and modernity, antinomic binomial, the trade mark of epidemics. Each of the great distributions of microbes in the Western World have followed the movements of travelers and explorers. The microbe always comes from somewhere else. With the candles of Orvieto came the flea-carrying rats and the death-dealing microbe from China via the Orient. Biology explains this quite calmly, *a posteriori*. Here, today, the long chain of homosexual fraternity has led the AIDS virus from the tropics to the rest of the Western homosexual world.

AIDS and Medicine in Mutation

Medicine has been outstripped by AIDS, as it always has been outstripped by each new epidemic. For medicine, however, and long before AIDS, had come the seal of modern times: its ever closer links with scientific logic. From this rapprochement it had contracted the modern obligation* to gauge itself. When AIDS came, medicine's retrospective grip on itself has been doubled by the attention of the media cameras and the public ear. If there is anything modern about AIDS, it is the availability of whatever we know about it to the collectivity. Everything about AIDS—more than

---

*Since the eighteenth century, indeed, medicine has not left the "scientific banquet," but as a rule it is a generation behind what is most "modern."

we know, in fact. A phenomenon of our society, the televisual or telematic drives to *know more* exceed the context of AIDS. Today, there is no war that is not filmed as it is being fought. No refugee camp without its images. Beirut, the Falkland Islands, Nicaragua. We complain in France of not having seen enough of Afghanistan! Americans have had Korea and Vietnam, and they would have been deprived of information about Grenada. Protests. In New York, the AIDS mystery has become a wad of chewing gum masticated in front of the tiny screen at four in the morning, just before the 4:13 weather report. Everyone will know: good-bye, mystery; hello, terror. The will to knowledge, diabolic daughter of the century of light* (though at the time only candles), today explodes under the follow spots and off cathodic tubes.

AIDS à l'Américaine

The AIDS film is an international production on the scale of the media network. But the script is American and carries the cultural insignia of its origin. To tell, to make known, to announce the disease and death—to inform the patient of the medical procedures that will follow, to obtain his informed consent, to expose and to discuss while exposing—North America has its cultural features. The dramatization that results from this relation to discourse, to exposure—what sometimes for us, prudish and evasive Latins, assumes the quality of an obscene voyeurism—has been, from the start, the trade mark of AIDS à l'Américaine. Down to those candlelight processions, organized by the gays of New York City to stage and theatricalize, in the most human sense of the term, the violence and death which have befallen them. It is no laughing matter: it is their culture, their relation to the law and to death. We need only look at the masks children wear on Halloween to understand that

---

*The apprentice-devil Mephistopheles must learn from his master that Faust-the-Impervious is vulnerable to "the desire to know."

culture has its frontiers. After all, are not the best-made horror films either British or American?

In France, we had another tradition. To say nothing, to know nothing; a father protects us with his mysteries. With AIDS we have also imported the flamboyant mise en scène ("An epidemic is spreading like wildfire ...") that is specifically American. "Gay homosexuality" had given us the *Gai Pied*,* and in France we are beginning to speak, to say what we had been told not to say and not to see. This is cultural "modernity" for everyone, not only for medicine.

Medicine Disturbed

Medicine has been sucked up into this whirlwind that so brutally disturbs and exposes it. It is interrogated, it is asked for an accounting, it is questioned in the Chamber of Deputies, and its most visible leaders on the AIDS front are threatened in editorials written by gay patients who are becoming less and less patient. Medicine is learning to live with this novelty. Its "internal" techniques, proper to the institution, its terminology, its concepts—all this can henceforth be exposed. The media have caught doctors actually putting questions to each other concerning AIDS. Export of the acronym GRID—gay *related immuno deficiency*—to the mass public was actually a leak. This designation had only an *operational character*, condensing information according to which 96 percent of the patients were homosexuals. But the force of the pejorative or mythical connotations which carried this GRID on the one hand, the parceled-out character of the observation establishing the designation on the other, should have tempered its designators' semantic flegma. Knowing, as they must have known, that the GRID "effect" would overflow the corridors of "scientific" gatherings. Granted, doctors write in professional journals. But corporatistic privacy inherent to technical segregation has become an illusion. For what is written there can be read by

---

*A weekly paper, the French equivalent of *The Advocate*—*Gai Pied* also sounds, in French, like *guêpier*, whose figurative meaning is that of a *trap*, a *ruse*, literally a wasp nest.

everyone, the price paid for mass education that permits the normally literate to decipher all messages. Especially when they are expressed in ordinary language. To declare, as one responsible physician declared, that "science cannot exclude the possibility that ordinary social contacts such as those which occur in families may cause the transmission of AIDS" could not have merely "scientific" consequences. The modernity, perhaps not entirely negative, of these leaks beyond the sphere of peers implies new obligations for physicians, as for all those who have a public responsibility. The time of whispers is passing. Even Richard Nixon was not entitled to keep such murmurs to himself. No more mysteries, no more fathers—modernity is advancing.

In the fashion of soldiers in their military academies suddenly confronted with war, medicine has traversed, with AIDS, a difficult period. Paradigms too vast or totally unusable, fantastic or illusory conceptual constructions: at first the doctors at the front were totally disarmed. An uncomfortable position that may have caused some to lose their sang-froid as they set off on a ground warfare offensive. If AIDS is a disease intrinsic to the homosexual terrain, how can we deal with it, if not by extirpating homosexuality? The "morbid" terrain, primary cause of the disease—this is an old argument, in medicine as elsewhere, always ready to revive in an ever more elaborate form. AIDS has been the occasion for certain nostalgics to replay their genetic Wagnerism and to verify (!) that homosexual behavior was or was not summarily inherited according to Mendelian laws* (initially applied to sweet peas and butterflies).

Sperm and sodomy, blood and sex, cancer and sodomy. Metaphors of *Alien* have buzzed through many ears: "Sperm, that Trojan horse," the sodomite version of the Fifth Column, which undermines from within. "Immune paralysis" of homosexuals overloaded with iron (!), following the "micro-auto-transfusions" caused by sodomitic bleeding.†

---

*The answer is no; homosexuality is not "simply" genetic.

†Transfusion of blood in minute quantities from one subject to another is associated with a better tolerance of transplants. Whence the accepted hypothesis of an immuno-suppressor effect of mini-transfusions.

"Immune overload," microbic parable of the promiscuous marathons threatening to overflow into AIDS.

Certain immune anomalies among homosexuals, especially among so-called "passive homosexuals," have been regularly noted. These anomalies resemble, at the end of a dark tunnel, certain of the anomalies observed in AIDS. Whereupon everything will have been foreseen in the Bible: the homosexuals have the stigmas of sodomy in their immune blood. These stigmas are the first signs of an incipient AIDS.

A certain feminism—the word taken literally—alleged masculine fragility ("Such a predominance of men affected."), and certain "scientific" types sought a genetic link between homosexuality and AIDS, a resonance of the sex-linked "hereditary disease"* hitherto, however, never applied to sexuality.

The homosexual trap has revealed the thinness of the scientific skin supposed to protect the weakest parts of medical reasoning. At the table of modern science, medicine still sits on no more than a stool, thus keeping an opportune mobility for changes of setting which the exercise of its temporal contract sometimes requires. On the other hand, medicine exposes itself to certain slips, its nose in the dish of its contemporaries' myths. In which position the learned in their long robes sometimes resemble Molière's Dr. Diafoirus.

Waiting for Biology

The scientific machine and its right arm, biology, are futurist monsters, armed with technologies, swollen with computers, with DNA recombinant.... Viruses, molecules, cells, everything will be straightened out. But when? The computer coughs, the molecule jerks, and the cell dies. Five years, ten years ... a long time. The biologico-scientific brontosaurus, if it is to be effective, must pass through the field of successive interrogations, according to its own

---

*The so-called gender-linked diseases, such as hemophilia, affect only boys, never girls.

rules and its own tempo, in which each stage of progress is the source of a subsequent interrogation; "immediate" medical benefits are always accidental. The scientific machine, turning back on itself, shoots out splendid sparks, stellar or earthy, and medicine must glean its rightful share. But since it cannot grant itself that luxury of *time* which gives scientists their dandiacal airs (blue eyes fixed on the horizon of history), medicine makes use of whatever it can put between its ears. Science is its support, biology its cane, but it is not at their service. Informed of the deliberations of a gradual biology, it must set itself to work with other instruments meanwhile, without waiting for the great biological machinery to be unpacked.

What doctors know how to do best is to observe. Since the dawn of the discipline first gave birth to their procedure, they have learned to describe and to associate. In the anti-AIDS campaign, they have had occasion to venture into the field with their notes ready, their eyes peeled. The ready-to-wear paradigms of institutional research require enormous amounts of cross-checking in order to confront the present situation. Let them be readjusted then, but meanwhile, let the doctors use their *savoir-faire* to unearth the facts. The detective-doctors have their work cut out for them. In AIDS there is a place for whatever can be picked up—begged, borrowed, or stolen, in order to put together a coherent, if patchwork, story. Let us put down our stethoscopes and our too slowly productive test tubes and begin the investigation. First of all, the telephone, an absurd instrument of research, but a modern one. Let us get the anecdote, the information, the verification, and the cross-checking into circulation. And let the institution support them, as an army supports its scouts.

·Part Three·

AIDS: THE CLINICAL PICTURE

OVERALL DESCRIPTION OF THE DISEASE: THE COURSE OF AN INFECTION BY HTLV-III/LAV

AIDS RESULTS FROM AN INFECTION OF IMMUNE CELLS (THE T-LYM-phocytes) by a specific retrovirus, HTLV-III/LAV. This virus affects the functioning and survival of the immune cells. Just as hepatitis is a disease that results from an infection of the liver cells by certain "hepatropic" viruses, AIDS is the result of infections from at least one "lymphotropic" retrovirus. But unlike viral hepatitis, which in the great majority of cases undergoes a spontaneously favorable development, AIDS is a serious disease because it represents the evolved form of the lymphocyte infection from the specific virus. The immune deficiency symptoms appear only in an advanced phase of the infection, a stage where, no doubt, over 90 percent of the implicated cells are weakened or destroyed.

In each of us, lymphocytes are constantly occupied in preventing the multiplication of a microbian flora, a long series of infectious agents capable of living parasitically on the cells of various organs: lung cells, cells of the digestive tract, brain cells, etc. The lymphocytes of category T normally limit the imminent expansion of germs present in most of us. These microbes, when freed from the tutella of the T-lymphocytes, multiply and create infections in the various organs. These secondary infections produce symptoms, and the totality of the symptoms (syndrome) linked to these secondary infections constitutes in essence the signs of AIDS. The paradox of the designation AIDS (acquired immune deficiency syndrome) is that this acryonym refers to the ultimate or advanced *consequences* of an infection of the immune cells, and not to this infection itself.

The symptoms of the infection by the AIDS agent, a first or primary infection, often remain discreet. They may even be entirely lacking, so that the disease reveals itself only by the signs of the secondary infections. Today, three or four years of experience and observations have taught doctors to locate the symptoms corresponding to this primary infection whose manifestations can be discovered in the patient's history long before the secondary infections appear, if they should ever appear.

Mr. V. was a man of 38, a commercial artist in New York, of French origin; of robust constitution, professionally active and productive, he had had no major health problems until 1982. A homosexual who made occasional forays into heterosexuality, he had several times contracted certain infections of venereal origin, but he had been cured, as is common enough, after appropriate treatments (one case of syphilis in 1972, another in 1978; several episodes of gonoccocus infections—from agents of acute urethritis, or blennorrhea; a double intestinal infection from amoebas and from lamblias*). Since 1982 a group of symptoms had appeared suggesting a progressive disease. A tired feeling accounted for neither by professional difficulties nor by affective conflicts. Physical fatigue accompanied by psychic vulnerability and a depressive tendency, as well as by a noticeable diminution of sexual appetite. Conjointly, and without evident modification of his eating habits, Mr. V. began to lose weight. Five kilos in several months, and by the end of 1982, over a dozen. To this picture are added episodes of fever spread over several days, varying from 37.5 to 39° C. A few months later, the episodes of fever have assumed more spectacular aspects, with temperatures up to 40° C. On

---

*Amoebas are small alien cells rather widespread in tropical regions; they live in polluted water and can become parasites on the human intestine. Contamination usually occurs by ingestion of spoiled food products or on the occasion of oral contact with the rectal secretions of a subject carrying amoebas.

these occasions the fever is preceded, for a few moments or hours, by chills and shivering which is followed by profuse sweating accompanied by a defervescence as is the case with any high fever falling rapidly. These episodes of fever disappear spontaneously after a few days, leaving behind a certain degree of exhaustion and apathy. This general condition at first remains without medical explanation. Various diagnoses successively envisaged then rejected, including notably that of cancer of an internal organ, which could, as a matter of fact, provoke symptoms of this type.

In December 1982, the signs are completed: a persistent inability to swallow reveals a tongue and throat covered with a thick whitish coating, as well as spots of "thrush" all over the palatal arch. This is apparently the consequence of a buccal and esophageal infection from a microbe of a family of microscopic mushrooms: Candida albicans. Almost simultaneously Mr. V. experiences a breathlessness at the slightest efforts: climbing the stairs to his apartment, and a cough also appears, especially at night. A fever of around 38 to 39° C reappears, and upon the intensification of the respiratory symptoms, Mr. V. is hospitalized. The elements of the diagnosis then proceed to accumulate. Examination of the blood shows a profound diminution of the number of white cells, and in particular of the lymphocytes. An X-ray reveals figures compatible with a bilateral and widespread infection of both lungs. A more direct examination of his respiratory system is made by fibroscope and an oscillating system permitting washing (with a sterile liquid) and collection. The liquid of pulmonary "alveolar lavage," examined under the microscope, reveals, after special dyes, the presence of another microbe: pneumocystis carinii. Mr V. has AIDS, and antibiotic treatments against the pneumonia germ and that of the buccal infection are begun. In a few weeks they will be effective. Mr. V.'s general condition continues to improve; he regains one or two kilos; the respiratory difficulties and the candida infection of mouth and throat disappear, and he can leave the hospital. However, the anomalies of the white corpuscles do not relinquish. Mr. V. remains in a state of immune deficiency, with too few lymphocytes in his blood and an absence of reaction to intracutaneous injection of an extract of Candida albicans with which he was nonetheless infected. Cutaneous "anergy" and "lymphopenia" (lack of lymphocytes) indicate this state of deficiency, heralding possible new infections. Indeed, the fever which had disappeared for several months following treatment reappears in irregular episodes, without being spectacular. The intermittent cough is also not very bothersome, except occasionally at night. A herpes-virus infection appears in the perineal region and extends in a few weeks, despite local remedies, to the whole of the buttocks and perineal region. This extensive and uncomfortable herpes is the source of an intercurrent complication: a staphylococcus infection of the skin. New antibiotic treatments specifically active against these microbes will overcome these infections. In July 1983, Mr. V. can once again think of returning home. But signs of acute cerebral infection suddenly contradict this hoped-for respite. Mental confusion and obnubilation followed by a crisis of generalized epilepsy indicate the emergence of multiple abscesses in the brain. An external photograph taken with the help of a complex apparatus, the tomodensitometer, certifies this hypothesis. Mr. V. is taken at once to neurosurgery for an operation. The diagnosis of widespread infection from toxoplasma could be established here, but despite an antibiotic treatment for this development, Mr. V. did not survive.

This observation illustrates the morbid developments which lead to AIDS. The first part of the disease is related to the infection from HTLV-III/LAV: intermittent fever and weight loss are its symptoms. The second part is that of the so-called secondary infections, both in time and in their causes. They follow the gradual collapse of immunity, under the effect of the infection of the immune cells by HTLV-III/LAV.

The pharyngitis and throat pain were signs of an infection from Candida albicans, a widespread microorganism, but one which does not appear under this extensive and invasive aspect unless there are pronounced immune anomalies. The second secondary infection was a pulmonary infection from pneumocystis carinii, whose symptoms are breathlessness, coughing, and high fever. Herpes throughout the anal and perineal region is linked to the multiplication of a virus also widespread, responsible for localized infections of the external genital organs in men and women, in the absence of any immune deficiency. The exuberance of the herpetic infection in Mr. V. indicated the immune deficiency characteristic of AIDS. Ultimately Mr. V. succumbed to a fourth parasite, toxoplasma. Most often toxoplasmic infection remains latent in the majority of individuals. In Mr. V. it took the form of an infection spreading throughout the cerebral tissue. The totality of these endogenous* and assuredly commonplace germs are known as "opportunistic" germs, because they "profit" on immune deficiency to multiply and to create lesions never observed in subjects whose immune performance is normal.

Examinations of blood showed anomalies compatible with a diagnoses of AIDS already established by the conjunction of the preceding symptoms: diminution of the number of lymphocytes circulating in the blood, cutaneous anergy in response to candidine, an extract of the Candida albicans yeast by which he was infected. On the other hand, intestinal infections from "tropical" parasites such as amoebas, benign tropical diseases observed in our regions, were in no way indicative of AIDS. Not any more than the venereal infections by which Mr. V. had been little troubled.

Infections from Candida albicans, from pneumocystis carinii, from herpes virus and from toxoplasma, and their symptoms—such are in Mr. V. the signs of the acquired immune deficiency appearing several months after the symptoms of the underlying primary infection from HTLV-III/LAV.

Let us reconsider the example of infection from virus B hepatitis. Virus B "lives" in the digestive tract (mouth, rectum), the liver cells (hepatocytes), and circulates in the blood of an infected subject. It is transmitted to another subject during intimate contacts (buccal or rectal contamination by intimate secretions) or, less often, during a transfusion of contaminated blood. In a first phase, the virus remains

---

*Endogenous: literally "born inside." Endogenous microbes are present in everyone, but in limited numbers.

"latent": it multiplies slowly and without perceptible damage to the carrier, notably in the liver cells. At the end of a few weeks or months (from 6 to 18 months), the first symptoms of hepatitis may make their appearance: this is jaundice. Concurrently, the virus solicits other elements of the organism, notably the immune cells: fever, skin eruptions (such as urticaria), general fatigue, stiffness, etc. These symptoms do not necessarily appear in *all* virus B carriers. On the contrary, the majority experience only a temporary discomfort or do not even notice their condition. Then the virus is neutralized by the normal immune defenses and apparently eliminated from the organism. However, in a small number of individuals, virus B will persist and in some cases cause serious perturbations of liver cell functioning, likely to lead to a state of hepatic deficiency. Hepatic deficiency is the source of symptoms: fatigue, mental disturbance, bleeding, etc. This set totality of symptoms might have led to the denomination *A*cquired *H*epato-*D*eficiency *S*yndrome (AHDS*). By an analogy, thus, we can say that the acquired immune deficiency syndrome is the set of symptoms that result from serious perturbations of the functioning of the "immunity" cells (lymphocytes); AIDS can be the belated consequence of an infection from a virus that gradually alters the functioning of the T-cells.†. Before leading to this stage, the infection of the T-cells by the retrovirus may or may not be translated by a certain number of other symptoms.

---

*The best-known corollary of AHDS would be certain serious forms of cirrhosis; cirrhosis is, as a matter of fact, one of the serious expressions of a virus B infection. "Undeserved" cirrhoses, linked to the virus and not, as the moralizing qualifier suggests, to a "vice," though one that indeed produces cirrhosis: alcoholism.

†Akin to infection of liver cells by hepatitis B virus which *sometimes* lead to cirrhosis, infection of immune cells by HTLV-III/LAV can *sometimes* lead to AIDS. At the AIDS phase the organs representing the immune system—lymph nodes, for instance—are *scarred,* as is the liver in cirrhosis.

· 2 ·

EARLY SYMPTOMS OF
INFECTION BY HTLV-III/LAV

APPROXIMATELY HALF OF THE PATIENTS WHO HAVE AIDS WILL have experienced prior symptoms corresponding to the early consequences of an infection by HTLV-III/LAV. On the other hand, possibly *less than ten percent* of those carrying the virus will ever experience any symptoms at all. Finally, almost *none* of the early symptoms of HTLV-III/LAV infection can predict a development toward a full-blown AIDS. Thus, it is totally improper to label this early phase in HTLV-III/LAV infection as "pre-AIDS." Indeed, most of those with such early symptoms will NOT evolve to AIDS. Also, of importance to the understanding of the medical procedures and uncertainties at the early stage of infection, there are no signs individually specific for an HTL-III/LAV infection. None, except Kaposi's sarcoma.

Nonspecific Symptoms

There are six of these: fever and night sweats; general fatigue and loss of libido; diarrhea; weight loss; superficial ganglia; and ordinary cutaneous lesions.

FEVER AND NIGHT SWEATS These are febrile intervals of low temperature (less than 39° C) spread over several days, then disappearing spontaneously, only to reappear, unpredictably, some weeks or months later. I.e., an unspectacular fever, capricious, shifting through spaced-out ups and downs. Sudden onsets of night sweats may accompany these febrile states or may survene without fever, sometimes serious enough to wet the bedclothes. These two symptoms are common to many infections or affections. Many of us have episodes of flu one or more times a year. Only the too-frequent repetition of such episodes or their unaccustomed duration—over more than a week—can indicate a persistent infection compatible but not synonymous with an infection from HTLV-III.

GENERAL FATIGUE AND LOSS OF LIBIDO This is an unwonted feeling of tiredness, not to be explained by mere circumstance; physical and psychic fatigue will occur for irregular periods. Loss of sexual appetite is often noted. But who has not experienced such symptoms on the occasion of affective conflicts, of professional or "existential" difficulties? Further, numerous chronic or recurrent affections—"metabolic," endocrine, immunological, etc.—can give rise to signs of this same type. The persistence or lastingly felt discomfort of these symptoms requires consulting a physician.

DIARRHEA Everyone knows the subjective definition of diarrhea, whose objective signs are liquidity of the stool and frequency of elimination: several times a day and sometimes a dozen times a day. The causes, here too, can be many: from a simple intestinal "grippe" to organic lesions of the intestine; frequently "without cause," diarrhea can be linked to emotional or alimentary disturbances, journeys, not to mention parasites and many other generally benign affections. The inaugural diarrhea of the infection from HTLV-III insofar as it is linked to this virus, remains modest and transitory, in our climates. This is not the case in tropical zones.

WEIGHT LOSS Weight loss amounting to several kilos, representing up to 15 percent of the body weight before the disease and even more (10 kilos for an adult weighing 70 kilos, for instance). This emaciation chiefly affects muscle tissues and may account in part for the sense of physical fatigue. Weight loss is gradual, for instance 5 kilos in several months, and is not linked to a patent modification of eating patterns. Just as fever and fatigue are not specifics of the infection by the AIDS virus, many lasting affections or infections can cause a marked weight loss. However, such weight losses, when they are really involuntary, should lead to consultation.

SUPERFICIAL GLANDS   The superficial "glands" (lymph nodes) are located in the inguinal regions (the groin), the armpits, and the neck: behind the head at the base of the skull, on each side of the neck and in the hollows of the collarbone. They are usually impalpable. In a minority of subjects infected from HTLV-III/LAV "adenopathies" (swelling of the nodes) can develop. These swellings remain moderate and affect two glandular regions (for example, neck and armpits or neck and groin) or all three. In each region appear one or several hypertrophied nodes of over a centimeter in diameter. These adenopathies form slowly over several weeks, almost surreptitiously, or more rapidly when accompanied by a fever of the flu type. They may persist for weeks, months, even several years, with phases of more marked swelling, when they may become painful, alternating with periods of relative subsidence. Such adenopathies are far from being a sure sign of an infection by the AIDS retrovirus, as other microbes can also give rise to chronic or long-lasting lymph-node swellings. However, the conjunction of superficial lymphadenopathies with certain skin lesions, eventually associated with any of the preceding constituent signs, will reinforce the probability of an underlying infection by HTLV-III/LAV.

ORDINARY CUTANEOUS LESIONS   A whole series of minor skin anomalies can appear in direct or indirect relation to the infection from the AIDS virus. Taken in isolation, without other associated symptoms, they are most insignificant in regard to HTLV-

III infection. On the contrary, in a subject presenting two or three of the five nonspecific precocious symptoms, these usually quite commonplace lesions can sustain a *suspicion* of HTLV-III/LAV infection: lesions from scratching, sometimes resembling urticaria, sometimes insect bites (prurigo); dryness of the skin of the legs and forearms; irritation of the skin of the face (seborrheic dermatitis); ordinary cutaneous infections of the overinfected acne type (pyodermatitis); "zonas" (lesions in the form of small blisters, followed by the formation of scabs, occurring in a cutaneous region correponding to one or several territories of superficial nerves). These zonas develop in time and extent like the classic zonas observed apart from AIDS and its virus.

The totality of these signs, when they are associated in one and the same subject, suggest an infection from the AIDS virus.

Kaposi's Sarcoma

This is certainly an early manifestation of infection from the HTLV-III/LAV retrovirus. Kaposi's sarcoma is most of all a cutaneous affection. It consists of patches or small nodules of a dark, purplish color appearing on the skin. The lesions are, generally, numerous: more than four or five, scattered over the body (torso, limbs, and sometimes even the face), appearing, as a rule, without pain or discomfort other than aesthetic or psychological. The purplish patches or spots can be found on the digestive mucous membranes: on the palate, in the mouth, in the intestines (where they can be observed directly by fibroscope) and on the rectum walls. Kaposi's sarcoma can affect other organs—for instance the lungs, the heart, the liver, but more often the lymph nodes.

Is the discovery of a Kaposi's-type lesion on the skin invariably the sign of an infection from HTLV-III/LAV? No. Kaposi's sarcoma was known long before AIDS existed in our countries. It is observed—an exceptional disease, moreover—in older subjects of Mediterranean descent: Italians, Greeks, Jews, Armenians, Turks.

Kaposi's sarcoma linked to an infection from the AIDS retrovirus is different from this classic Kaposi's: the cutaneous, Kaposi's Sarcoma are rare or localized; in the form linked to HTLV-III/LAV, new lesions will often appear on other parts of the body or enlarge on the spot into broader patches, whereas classic Kaposi's sarcoma is usually "tranquil." But these indications do not suffice to ascertain whether limited spots of Kaposi-type lesions are indeed relatable to an infection by HLTV-III/LAV. Certainly, numerous Kaposi lesions in a young man is almost unequivocally linked to such an infection.* The following two observations underline these different aspects of a disease with a single name, Kaposi's sarcoma, equivocal as to its position with regard to infection from the AIDS virus.

OBSERVATION NO. 1

Monsieur B., age 32, French, bisexual, without distinctive medical past (3 blennorhas), finds a number of tiny purplish specks appearing on his face during the second quarter of 1981; analogous lesions appear on his palate, tonsils, and pharynx, and the fibroscope discovers similar ones on the intestine. One of the cutaneous lesions is removed by local anesthesia for microscopic examination (histologic examination). Kaposi's sarcoma, the histologist reports. Final diagnosis: widespread Kaposi's sarcoma, suspicion of infection by the AIDS virus. Subsequent developments of the disease will confirm this likelihood. A classic anti–Kaposi's sarcoma treatment will not prevent the appearance of new Kaposi's-type nodules on the face, thorax, and limbs during the first months of 1982, when there also appears a Candida infection in the mouth; buccal and perineal herpes, associated with a great weight loss (12 kilos in 6 months). In June 1982, the condition changes, a high fever occurs in connection with a bilateral pneumonia due to a herpes virus leading to death despite treatment.

---

*In subjects receiving no medication likely to diminish immune performance.

OBSERVATION NO. 2

Monsieur P., age 36, without notable medical antecedents, consults in December 1981 for small sensitive purplish nodules appearing on the soles of both feet over several weeks. One of these nodules, when removed, reveals under the microscope a typical aspect of Kaposi's sarcoma. Inspection of the digestive mucous membrane by direct endoscopic examination indicates no lesion. Final diagnosis: localized Kaposi's sarcoma without other anomalies. The lesions, as is habitual, are given radiation treatment and generally disappear. For 39 months, Monsieur P. has been feeling well, with the occasional appearance of a nodule on one foot or the other, which are removed by microscopic surgical intervention. There is no Mediterranean ancestry in his family, and he has never been in either Africa or America. Monsieur P. has all the signs of a classical Kaposi's syndrome, and in his case there is no objective reason to envisage an infection from the AIDS virus. Monsieur P.'s homosexuality is not synonymous to AIDS virus infection.

Outcome of the HTLV-III/LAV Infection

Specific, like the lesions of the scattered Kaposi-Type, or non-specific, such as fever, diarrhic episodes, attacks of fever, weight loss, glands, all these symptoms may appear relatively early in the course of an infection by HTLV-III/LAV. Is development in the direction of AIDS inevitable? At what rate?

Even before one could detect the virus's presence, experience with patients presenting with such early symptoms had taught us that intermittent diarrhea, high fevers, swollen superficial nodes, could spontaneously disappear without our really being able to tell whether or not it was a cured infection to the then putative virus.

Development from early infection to AIDS is rare and capricious, as the slowness and the unpredictability of the process of immune destruction by the retrovirus might lead us to suppose. Further, we have observed periods of spontaneous remission, if not of cure: diminution in volume of the hypertrophied glands, weight gain of several kilos, sometimes very prolonged disappearance of fever and diarrhea. The transition to a confirmed AIDS can take several months or years, sometimes less—this remains difficult to anticipate, for we do not yet have the means to make predictions in individual cases. On this point, infection from HTLV-III/LAV resembles other diseases from persistent viruses. Having discovered the virus has not by itself taught us to establish the ultimate gravity or benignity of the infection. Only continuous observation permits the doctor to inform his individual patient of the development of his disease, with some help from biological tests.

3

LATER SYMPTOMS OF THE INFECTION BY HTLV-III/LAV

Secondary Infections

IN AN UNFORESEEABLE INTERVAL—FROM SEVERAL MONTHS TO TWO or three years—a *certain number* of patients (between 1 and 10 percent?) develop a state of extreme immune deficiency whose unequivocal sign appears as serious secondary infections. The symptoms of these are as varied as the infections themselves. They depend essentially on the localization of the microbes in a specific organism. Further, the infections are associated with one another or follow one another in the same patient. The description of all the symptoms of a recognized case of AIDS would fill the equivalent of half a dictionary of infectious diseases. In the advanced form of the disease—at the immune deficiency stage—the germs involved are most endogenous microbes, latent parasites present in small numbers within a normal host. We may notice, as well, certain environmental germs, varying according to the regions of the world the patient happens to be in at the time his AIDS develops. The following chart lists the germs found and the main diseases that have resulted from them:

GERMS	SYNDROMES
Bacteria	
• mycobacteria	scattered or atypical tuberculosis
Hominis	
Avium	
Intracellular	
• salmonellas	septicemias, cerebral abscess, intestinal
Typhi murium	infections
Dublin	
Legionella	pneumonia
Protozoa	
• pneumocystic carinii	diffuse pneumonias
• cryptosporidium	intestinal infections (chronic diarrheas)
• isospora belli	intestinal infections
• toxoplasma	scattered cerebral absesses
• leishmania donovani	spleen and bone marrow infections
Yeasts	
• Candida albicans	bucco-esophagial infections
• Cryptococcus neoformans	meningitis, scattered infections
• Histoplasma capsulatum	scattered infections (bone marrow, lungs, skin, lymph nodes)
• Nocardia asteroides	cerebral abscess, pulmonary infections
• Aspergillus fumigatus	pulmonary infections
Viruses	
• cytomegalic virus	chronic pneumonia, retinitis, lack of bone marrow
• herpes simplex I	Kaposi's syndrome
• herpes simplex II	necrotizing ulcerations
	• peribuccal
	• perigenital
	prolonged and/or extensive zonas
• varicella-zona	Burkitt's lymphoma*
• Epstein-Barr	progressive encephalitis, superficial warts
• papovavirus	

Non-limitative list of germs causing secondary infections in AIDS sufferers.

*See p. 129, chapter 5: Understanding the Symptoms of the Disease.

Which Development?

The period of secondary infections marks a turning point in the natural history of the disease in a given subject. The profound immune deficiency heralded by these infections implies the loss of the defense systems, and thereby the possibility of recurrences of infections from one germ after another. But there remains a share of unknown factors, as to the real *degree* of immune deficiency. Elsewhere, anecdotal but undeniable observations reveal that after a first or second infection, certain patients experience phases of prolonged respite. These "remissions" occur unexpectedly and are of unpredictable duration. These facts must incite patients and physicians to continue their efforts in fighting secondary infections. Especially since advances can be made in this realm, as a consequence of better knowledge of the disease and more sophisticated use of the existing antibiotic medicaments.

4

TESTS AND EXAMINATIONS INDICATING AN INFECTION FROM HTLV-III/LAV

TWO SERIES OF TESTS EXIST. THOSE THAT PERMIT DETECTING IF A given subject, healthy or ill, is a virus *carrier*, and those that say if the infection from HTLV-III/LAV involves *disturbances* of lymphocyte performances and attempt to estimate their degree. Two orders of tests which furnish different information, though rigorously complementary and indispensable, with their respective limits. As a matter of fact, when we can say of an individual that he is a carrier of the virus, we have as yet specified nothing of the gravity of the infection's consequences. Now, the only question which the subject thus stigmatized would then ask is: Is it serious—will it become serious? Does infection from HTLV-III/LAV involve an immune deficiency, whether mild, serious, or mortal? Tests evaluating the degree of immune deficiency, *before* secondary infections from opportunistic germs indicate the immunitary ravages the virus has perpetrated, are and remain essential. (A renal disease is serious when it destroys more than 95 percent of kidney functions: renal insufficiency. Infection from HTLV-III/LAV is probably serious when it destroys more than 95 percent of the T4-lymphocyte functions: immune insufficiency or immune deficiency.)

Other tests show the HTLV-III/LAV "solicits" the immune system before "destroying" it. These tests do not have much practical utility for the sufferers but we can foresee that tomorrow they might provide important information.

Direct Tests

The identification of the AIDS virus as HTLV-III/LAV has officially been recognized. Hence through biological testing it has become possible to recognize who is a carrier of the virus and who is not. To do this two methods are presently used: cytocultures and antibody testing. Cytoculture starts from specimen of the individual's blood, bone marrow, lymph node, sperm, saliva, all containing T-lymphocytes, some of which are presumably infected with HTLV-III/LAV. The virus-harboring, "permissive" T-cells are induced to multiplication, so providing the incentives for the virus to also multiply. Electron microscopy done on the growing cells, chemical analysis of the medium in which the T-cells (and the searched virus) are replicating, including nucleic acid probing by sophisticated methods, may lead to the isolation and identification of the HTLV-III/LAV from T-cells of one infected individual. These techniques are highly cumbersome, however. Detecting antibodies against HTLV-III/LAV in the serum of a person infected from it is far easier and faster—it is also more sensitive and successful in that 95 percent of patients with AIDS so tested have been shown to have such specific anti-HTLV-III/LAV antibodies in their serum. Growing the virus from the T-cells of the patients yield much less consistent positive results, due to technical pitfalls. It is obvious that without modifying the immediate therapeutic possibilities, this information affords additional elements for diagnosis. The example of infections from the hepatotropic viruses (virus A, virus B, virus non A–non B) emphasizes the considerable help given doctors by the identification of a virus and the possibility of proving its presence in a given subject. Beyond this justified enthusiasm, we must keep in mind the *medical limit* of the direct tests for infection: the presence of HTLV-III/LAV in a subject gives no indication as to the gravity of the viral infection.

Indirect Tests

We can examine by microscope a tissue fragment taken under local anesthesia: hypertrophied ganglion or Kaposi's sarcoma lesion. The biopsy (microscopic examination of a biological specimen: "bioopsis") gives indirect but useful indices of an infection from HTLV-III/LAV.

BIOPSY OF A KAPOSI'S SARCOMA LESION

The purplish nodules and patches have this aspect because they reproduce distorted images of the capillaries. The cells which normally construct and delimit the capillary wall (endothelial cells) have multiplied locally; with them, the fibroblasts, another type of cells which surround the capillaries, have also proliferated. This double proliferation, in variable relative proportions from one case to another, presents what is called a "sarcoma" aspect—tumors constituted of fibroblastic cells. But this optical analogy, if it has given rise to the designation Kaposi's sarcoma, is only an *image*. Kaposi's sarcoma has few elements in common with a "true" sarcoma, a rapidly proliferative tumor of high malignity, giving rise to the extremely rapid dissemination of metastases in bones, lungs, and liver. Kaposi's sarcoma is, in most cases, different; its scattered lesions, frequent in AIDS, are not metastases in the true sense. This semantic difference covers the following biological reality: the endothelial and fibroblastic cells of the Kaposi's sarcoma are less rapidly proliferative than the cells of a true sarcoma. A nuance that is more than a nuance if we compare the survival period of a true sarcoma with the distinctly more favorable survival of patients with the Kaposi's sarcoma. And in most AIDS cases, mortality is lower in subjects whose first sign was Kaposi's syndrome, in relation to those whose infection by opportunistic germs was the initial symptom.

Is the Kaposi's sarcoma lesion the sign of an infection by HTL-VIII/LAV? Yes, no doubt it is when the lesions are scattered over the skin, in a young subject, and when there exist profound lymphocyte disturbances or, *a fortiori*, one or several secondary infections. Not necessarily so, if the lesions are rare, localized, and isolated, without lymphocyte anomalies.

BIOPSY OF A LYMPH NODE

The infection from HTLV-III/LAV is one of the viral infections capable of producing swollen lymph nodes (lymphadenopathy). Such swellings are the palpable translation of some of the effects of these viruses on the lymphocyte cells. The viruses solicit them intensely and, doing so, set off their multiplication. The number of lymphocytes increases in the node which becomes hypertrophied: palpable lymphodenopathy.

In the early stage of infection by the retrovirus, when there exist palpable lymph nodes (which is true of only about 30 to 50 percent of the cases), biopsy of the ganglion shows certain cells (lymphocytes, macrophages) in greater number. All classes of lymphocytes circulating in the blood are represented in the node, in proportions crudely comparable. In these nodes, as in the blood, T8-lymphocytes* predominate over the T4-lymphocytes under the stimulating effect of the viruses which "engage" those T8-cells in preference to T4-cells. These nonspecific indications do not in themselves permit us to implicate HTLV-III/LAV. Certain nuances suggest calling attention to them, however: the intensity of the lymphocyte stimulation itself, the more marked development of the capillaries and of their constitutive cells, the endothelial cells.

Beyond these fine points, three anomalies can mark more distinctly, but still indirectly, the trail of the AIDS virus: Kaposi's sarcoma lesions; an exuberant proliferation of class-B lymphocytes; or a partial shrinking of certain regions of the node.

KAPOSI'S SARCOMA LESIONS IN THE NODE   In the actual absence of visible lesions on the skin, the biopsied node can present Kaposi's sarcoma lesions with the double proliferation of endothelial

---

*Cf. p. 123.

and fibroblastic cells. Just as the lesions of Kaposi's sarcoma scattered on the skin represent, in a young subject, the indirect sign of a probable infection from HTLV-III/LAV, lesions of this type in a hypertrophied node have an identical signification.

EXUBERANT PROLIFERATION OF CLASS-B LYMPHO-CYTES*   A limited number of AIDS patients have presented an aspect of this type in their nodes.

PARTIAL SHRINKING OF THE GANGLION IN CERTAIN ZONES   Infection by HTLV-III/LAV leads, in the worst eventuality, to a major diminution of the T4-lymphocytes in the blood. This development may find its counterpart on the level of a still-hypertrophied ganglion. In this case, the biopsy reveals certain areas of "atrophy" in regions where T4-lymphocytes usually lodge and accumulate. These aspects testify to an already advanced development in the history of the infection from the AIDS virus. They herald, for the weeks or months to come, the strictly speaking AIDS stage of the infection from the retrovirus, with the threat of secondary infections by opportunistic germs. Thus, tissue samples can help the physician to designate the infection from the AIDS virus indirectly and sometimes to estimate the degree of lymphocyte damage.

Tests Evaluating the Degree of Immune Deficiency

CUTANEOUS TESTS   In Monsieur B., the introduction of candidine under the skin did not induce the expected reaction in a subject presenting a Candida infection. This anergy (the absence of reaction) was the indication of a profound deterioration of the T-lymphocytes.

---

*The lymphocyte cells are in the blood and the lymph nodes in the proportion of 1/5 to 2/5 of class B, the rest being of class T.

SIGNIFICATION OF CUTANEOUS TESTS IN GENERAL   The cutaneous tests consist in introducing, by very delicate and very superficial injections, micro-quantities of certain substances extracted from microbes. Conveniently, the extracts come from microbes that most of us have "met" before: mumps virus, Candida albicans (candidin), streptococci, tetanus bacilli, etc.

Our organism sustains a collection of immune cells, a "pool" of lymphocytes sensitive to most of these extracts. Confronted with these "antigens", the lymphocytes are solicited. They "react" to these "recall" antigens. Hence we artificially introduce by injection or superficial micro-incision one or another or several of these microbial antigens into the skin. The sensitive lymphocytes, which circulate continually between the blood and the lymph, percolate through the tissues toward the site of the injection. They "recognize" the substances introduced and "react" to their contact. They multiply to greater numbers and, concurrently, release into their micro-environment certain soluble substances, the "lymphokines." These natural chemical substances are hormones with a short radius of action. They act on other nearby cells (notably the macrophages) which they attract there, where the lymphocytes and the microbial substance have encountered each other.

The little dark-red induration which appears clearly (26 to 48 hours later) at the site of the intra-dermic injection of microbic extracts visibly and palpably translates this group of cellular movements: local afflux of "secreting" lymphocytes and of their auxiliaries the macrophages. In order to develop according to this scenario, the cutaneous reaction implies that the sensitive lymphocytes are simultaneously capable of percolating through the tissues toward the skin, of being there in sufficient number, and of fulfilling their secretory function there. In order to do this, the cells must be intrinsically healthy and not prevented from acting.

The absence of reaction—cutaneous anergy—in Monsieur B. indicated a profound alteration of the T-lymphocytes by HTLV-III/LAV. In him, as in the majority of those in whom the viral infection has reached the AIDS stage, the T4-lymphocytes are rare and weakened.

Does this mean that destroyed cutaneous reactions always signify a state of profound deficiency in the number and performances of T4-cells? Certainly not. Indeed, cutaneous anergy is often observed in the early phase of the HTLV-III/LAV infection, whereas the latter has not yet caused any serious failure of the T4-cells. In the same way, an anergy of this type is observed in benign viral infections such as measles or mumps. Cutaneous anergy is among the signs of numerous viral infections. Infection from HTLV-III/LAV shares this sign with them. In fact, viruses provoke, in these cases, the production of interference factors that could modify the capacity of the T4-cells to perform their functions.

Cutaneous anergy can therefore also be the sign of an infection from certain viruses (and notably from HTLV-III/LAV) without there being that profound immune deficiency that *only* the AIDS virus inflicts. Cutaneous anergy is an overall test. Interpretation of its results is, as we see, ambiguous.

THE LYMPHOCYTE COUNT   A blood sample is sufficient to make a count of the lymphocytes in circulation. At the AIDS stage, this number is frankly diminished (below 1,000 per microliter of blood).

THE "LYMPHOCYTE DIFFERENTIAL" (THE ABSOLUTE AND RELATIVE NUMBERS OF T4-AND T8-LYMPHOCYTES) Within the entire class of the T-lymphocytes of the blood, there exist two unequal subgroups, the group of T4-lymphocytes and the group of T8-lymphocytes, in the average ratio of two T4 to one T8, but with considerable physiological variations in these proportions. Infection by HTLV-III/LAV ultimately leads to a profound diminution in the absolute number of T4-lymphocytes. This observation however is made *late* in the course of the viral infection. At an earlier stage, the number of T4-lymphocytes circulating in the blood is not diminished, but the number of T8-lymphocytes can be augmented. This immunological anomaly is again not specific to HTLV-III/LAV infections. Like cutaneous anergy, it is induced by numerous viruses that have the property of soliciting T8-cells "in preference" to T4-cells. The increase in the number of T8-cells in relation to T4-cells causes an authentic lowering of the T4/T8 proportion. As in the case of cutaneous anergy, the lowering of this ratio (normally of 2 ± 1, here of .5 to 1) is therefore not necessarily the signature of a profound immune deficiency, although in the final stage of AIDS this ratio is modified downward, by reason of the spectacular reduction in the number of T4-cells.

EVALUATION OF THE LYMPHOCYTE FUNCTIONS IN CYTOCULTURE Many systems permit questioning *in vitro* the performances of lymphocytes from blood taken in sufficient quantities from the patient and separated from other elements of the blood: multiplication function of the stimulated cells, secretion function, cytotoxic function.* These functions depend, among others, on the number and the quality of the T4-cells. They are, on the whole, diminished in the AIDS stage. The technological cost of these investigations is not, in most cases, justified by the quantity of information they yield beyond those provided by the preceding examinations and the clinical elements. Their informative values may be refined in the future so as to permit exteriorization of anomalies at a less caricatural stage.

On this point, numerous tests indicate or suggest that in the early phase of the infection, the immune cells and the macrophages are strongly "solicited" and "reactive" before showing immune collapse at the AIDS stage. Although they have not as yet given proof of their diagnostic interest, or even for the most part of their predictive value, they instruct us as to the immunological modifications provoked by HTLV-III/LAV. With regard to future research and investigation, they deserve to be presented and discussed.

---

*Certain lymphocyte cells express a toxic activity against other cells which are "offered" to them as a target.

FURTHER INDICES OF IMMUNOLOGICAL SOLICITATIONS

Signs of Increased Lymphocyte Activity   The class-B lymphocytes represent the other class of immune cells beside T-cells. Their function is to secrete certain chemical substances known as "immuno-globulins" (the classical antibodies). Often patients have a high level of these substances in their blood. And their B-lymphocytes, put in culture, show an unwonted propensity to multiply.

The relation with infection by HTLV-III/LAV is not immediate. HTLV-III/LAV, in principle, infects T-cells and not normal B-cells. The B-cells and the production of antibodies are *relatively* "spared" in the course of the viral infection, including the phase of immune collapse which massively affects the T4-cells. But a physiological link exists between those two cell types.

B-cells and T4-cells   The T4-cells secrete lymphokines* when they are stimulated. Among these lymphokines, we know certain factors stimulating B-cell growth. The hyperactivism of B-cells in HTLV-III/LAV infections might indirectly reflect a state of accentuated activity of the T4-lymphocytes. And since the B-cell anomalies persist even in the advanced phase of AIDS, we must suppose that despite the collapse of T-cells at this stage, at least some T-cells continue to produce factors stimulating the growth of B-cells. A paradox which other related anomalies, such as the hypersecretion of T4-lymphocytes in AIDS, may help to sustain.

Presence in the Patients' Blood of High Quantities of Interferons   Alpha interferons are natural substances produced among other cells by macrophage and T lymphocytes, in response to the viral infection. The secretion of alpha interferons is potentialized by the "activation" of the same macrophages under the effect of certain lymphokines, secreted, let us remember, by T4-lymphocytes.

Presence in the Patients' Blood of High Quantities of Beta-2-Microglobulin
This is a protein widespread on the surface of every cell in the

---

*Natural chemical substances secreted by the T4-cells: these are hormones with a short radius of action.

organism. It is produced and "salted out" in the environment of the cell in increased quantities when the cells have been in contact with increased quantities of interferons.

Presence in the Patients' Urine of Free Neopterine in High Quantities Neopterine is a natural chemical composite produced by the macrophages under the effect of direct (virus in the cell) or indirect stimulations, especially when the macrophages have been "activated" in their functions by imbibing "activating" lymphokines.

These anomalies are not in themselves rigorously specific for HTLV-III/LAV infection. But they have at least one element of coherence: the secretory activity of T4-cells. Numerous viral infections, without special tropism for the immune cells, nonetheless have stimulation effects comparable, even identical, to those we have just described: alpha interferons in the blood, excretion of free neopterine, stimulation of class-B lymphocytes. As a matter of fact, many viruses, such as that of German measles, infectious mononucleosis, and a number of others as well, "engage" the functioning of T4-cells.*

These viruses represent elements alien to the organism, and the T4-lymphocytes are normally stimulated when alien substances are "presented" to them.

In infections by HTLV-III/LAV, the same biological effects may derive from the same immunological causes: cells are infected with the retrovirus; the parasite virus exposes its "alien" constituents to the surface of the infected cells. Other T4-cells, not infected, collect these alien structures, as do anti-cytomegalic T4-cells, anti-measles T4-cells, etc. Hence there must exist anti-HTLV-III/LAV T4-cells, spotting the retrovirus on the surface of other T4-cells infected by the virus. This stimulation would conform to the laws of immune biology. The T4-cells, immune cells, merely react to what they "perceive" as alien, from the "exterior." The substances secreted (the lymphokines) would, from this point of view, be the witness of this physiological

---

*However, "engagement" of T4-cells is less marked than that of T8-cells, judging by their more marked multiplication than that of T4-cells.

immune engagement. But another more attractive hypothesis suggests itself. It integrates what we already know about the retrovirus (it infects the T4-cells) with a new fact: *the persistence of the "signs of nonspecific viral infection"* is particular to AIDS.

Alpha interferons, beta-2-microglobulin, stimulation of B-cells: these signs, compatible with an engagement of T4-cells, are prolonged in HTLV-III/LAV infections, whereas they disappear in the other infections.

This notion of time suggests that, contrary to these other viruses, HTLV-III/LAV *lastingly* infects the organism which, in these cases at least, does not get rid of them. The infection seems lasting and active, in the sense in which it lengthily sustains these signs of immunological solicitations. Can we suppose that the biological signs of engagement of T4-cells testify to a prolonged stimulation of T4-cells reacting against other T4-cells infected by the virus? No doubt, but since the virus is a parasite *from within* upon at least a certain number of T4-cells, why not suppose that the viral parasite modifies the functions of the T-cells *from within*? As long as there is a sufficient number of T4-cells modified from within, would we not see the biological anomalies persist?

Now, the AIDS virus has the features of a member of the HTLV family. A retrovirus capable of being integrated into the nucleus, in the nucleic acids of T4-cells. A virus family about which we know that the first isolated specimen in history (HTLV-I) can "transform" T4-cells into cancerous cells, perhaps by making the cell massively produce natural substances normally secreted in weak quantities. Hence we might postulate that HTLV-III "transforms" a *small number* of T4-cells into secretory cells—cells secreting hormonal substances not directly cancerigenic for the T4-cells.

The persistence of the biological signs of immune engagement would translate not a stimulation "exterior" to the T4-cells, but "interior" modifications proper to infected cells. This hypothesis would have the further merit of explaining why these "secretory" anomalies seem to persist at the advanced stage of infection from the AIDS virus—a stage where, in fact, there remain only very few healthy T4-cells capable of reacting physiologically to the presence of alien microbes.

· 5 ·

UNDERSTANDING THE
SYMPTOMS OF THE DISEASE

Fever, Fatigue, Weight Loss, Swollen Lymph Nodes

THESE SYMPTOMS SEEM TO BE THE CONSEQUENCE OF THE SOLICITA-
tions made by the AIDS virus on the immune system. The nodes
are enlarged and palpable because they contain more cells, in reaction
to stimulation by the viral infection. The stimulated cells—
white corpuscles which are also found in the blood (macrophage-
monocytes, lymphocytes)—multiply and secrete into the organism
certain "natural" substances in greater quantity: among the latter,
endopyrogenes and alpha interferons.

ENDOPYROGENES

These are chemical substances whose origin and composition we
know precisely. They upset the thermostat within the brain, whose
responsibility is to keep our temperature at around 37° C. Under
their action, fever rises to around 38° to 39° C, as in a number of
microbic infections or certain cancers. These substances also participate in muscular dissolution. They increase the dissipation by the
muscle cells of their protein capital; they concurrently diminish their

capacity to "reconstruct muscle" by limiting their multiplication (catabolic effect). Weight loss due to AIDS may be linked to this catabolic effect of the endopyrogenes on the muscles.

ALPHA INTERFERONS

These natural substances are produced by macrophage cells whose white blood corpuscle relative is the monocyte.* Interferons produce states of general fatigue, physical as much as psychic, sometimes of unusual intensity. This is also indicated by certain sufferers, outside of AIDS, who have received treatment involving high doses of interferons. The psychic constituent is sometimes accompanied by a depressive state, reversible upon cessation of treatment. The chemical explanation of this psychic symptom may be as follows: the alpha interferon has a structural relationship with another natural substance secreted by the cerebral cells, endorphine beta. The endorphines represent the natural and endogenous counterpart of morphine and other opium derivatives. The endorphines have effects on pain and certain psychic consequences very different from those of morphine. The sensation of general fatigue and the sometimes depressive tendency of subjects infected by HTLV-III/LAV in its initial phase might be linked to the endogenous production of alpha interferons with pseudo- or para-endorphinic effects. These nonspecific symptoms might translate the immune "reaction" to the presence of HTLV-III/LAV. But, if they are distressing, they also might express some form of "resistance" to the infectious agent. The stimulated immune cells may struggle against the virus itself or its damaging effects on T-cells. As a matter of fact, we note that only a small number of people having palpable lymph nodes have an unfavorable development—as if the organism's reaction, clamorous since it involves symptoms, managed to limit the viral infection or to prevent its most harmful effects (destruction of T4-cells).

These symptoms are common to various diseases implicating the participation of the lymphatic system. Certain infections, such as tuberculosis,

---

*The white corpuscles of the blood are constituted, among others, of lymphocytes and monocytes.

diseases like Hodgkin's disease (a cancer of the lymphatic system), and other affections, unrelated to an infection by the AIDS virus, share with it certain common signs: weight loss, fatigue, fever, night sweats. These diseases also involve an increased production of natural substances secreted by the immune cells. Hence we must not consider these signs as certain indications of an infection from the AIDS virus, but as those of a perhaps "lymphatic" infection or affection still to be identified.

Kaposi's Disease

IS KAPOSI'S SARCOMA A CANCER?

This question is fraught with a series of implications, given the emotional and phantasmatic value of the designation "cancer." One can give at least two operational definitions of a cancer. *The definition of cellular biology*: an assemblage of cells of a certain type from a certain organ, having initially experienced a number of genetic events, so that the cell is "transformed"; the cell multiplies in preference to others and gives rise to tumors by accumulation of proliferating cells. *The clinical and prognostic definition:* tumors, capable in the worst cases of growing rapidly, of producing metastases in various organs, susceptible of causing death within relatively short periods.

In AIDS, the Kaposi's sarcoma does not readily fit either of these categories. The cells that proliferate in Kaposi's sarcoma are not transformed as leukemia cells would be, for example; hitherto it has been difficult to obtain cells from Kaposi's sarcoma that would perpetuate themselves in culture in a continous fashion, as do the transformed "cancerous" cells. Local growth of Kaposi's sarcoma tumors is often slow and "modest." Excrescent tumors deforming a limb are rarely seen. The distress caused by Kaposi's sarcoma is often of a merely aesthetic order, when its many lesions affect the visible parts of the body and especially the face. This eventuality is rare.

The dissemination of cutaneous lesions, if it does fit the definition of AIDS–Kaposi's sarcoma, does not consist of metastases, but rather of an initial dissemination of lesions. This does not indicate that the disease has spread, contrary to what dissemination implies in those cancers of such organs as the lungs, pancreas, or testicles. This difference results from the fact that Kaposi's sarcoma cannot be compared to an organ cancer. As for the prognosis, statistics going back to the start of the AIDS epidemic testify to the relatively favorable character of the Kaposi's sarcoma compared to the more frequently and more rapidly fatal development of AIDS cases with infections from opportunistic germs. The seriousness of AIDS–Kaposi's sarcoma derives first of all from the degree of immune deficiency that is ultimately associated with it. The Kaposi's sarcoma lesions without marked immune deficiency receive a more favorable prognosis.

With regard to the two definitions of cancer we have given, we should be rather inclined to answer: no, Kaposi's sarcoma is not "really" a cancer.

IS KAPOSI'S SARCOMA A DISEASE OF HOMOSEXUALS?

The epidemiological data are clear. Among all cases of AIDS, the cutaneous or lymph node Kaposi's sarcomas are 10 to 15 times more frequent in homosexuals as compared to male heterosexuals who have AIDS. Among all cases of AIDS–Kaposi's sarcoma, more than 90 percent concern homosexuals, whereas homosexuals today represent only 70 percent of AIDS cases. Why such a statistically indisputable association? Without taking up the argument of the general susceptibility of men* and only comparing homosexual and heterosexual men, the prevalence of Kaposi's sarcoma in homosexuals abides. Is there a biological link here between homosexuality and the Kaposi's sarcoma lesions? One, at least, suggests itself: persistent or repeated infections from the cytomegalic virus.

---

*"Classic," non-AIDS Kaposi's sarcoma is distinctly more frequent in men than in women.

Kaposi's Sarcoma and Cytomegalic Infections

Many investigations of the 1970's had shown an association between classical Kaposi's sarcoma (non-AIDS) and cytomegalic infections (CMV). Kaposi's sarcoma is constituted in part, as we have seen, of proliferating endothelial cells, the ones which line the capillaries. Now, the CMV lodges in these cells. And this virus has been found in lesions of Kaposi's sarcoma, starting from endothelial cells cultivated *in vitro*. Thus, Kaposi's sarcoma seems linked to the infection of endothelial cells by the cytomegalovirus. The infection, instead of leading to destruction, causes the *multiplication* of the parasite-attacked cell. Conversely, multiplication of the endothelial cell is favorable to that of the CMV.*

Homosexuals, it appears, excrete quantities of cytomegalic virus in their sperm. Objective observation of this fact has been made in various cities of the United States, especially New York and San Francisco. Special "susceptibility" of homosexuals to CMV infection? Probably not. The individual homosexual man happens to be reinfected each time that some exogenous virus is deposited on his mucous membrane (buccal or rectal); the subject, in his turn, infects his partner(s). Duality inherent in male homosexual activity, the contaminating secretions (sperm) are in turn given and received. Thus between masculine homosexuality and the infection of endothelial cells by the cytomegalic virus, there is merely a simple logic of microbes.

What are the ultimate relationships between Kaposi's sarcoma—linked to an infection of endothelial cells by cytomegalovirus—and AIDS—resulting from an infection of T4-lymphocytes by HTLV-III/LAV? Kaposi's sarcoma, before AIDS, was known to develop not only among Mediterraneans but also in patients receiving immunosuppressive drugs. These medications are deliberately prescribed

---

*See p. 43.

because they interfere with the functions of T-lymphocytes. T-lymphocytes in the recipient host, if they were not impeded, would reject the graft. Immuno-deficiency created by such medications releases the endogenous cytomegaloviruses from the control which T-cells exert upon them. So, in graft recipients treated with immuno-suppressive drugs, CMV multiplies and so does the number of viral specimen within a given endothelial cell. This might also augment the "chances" of "cancerous" transformation to occur within the infected cell: Kaposi's sarcoma. In AIDS, T-lymphocytes malfunctions are well documented, Kaposi's sarcoma being a mere consequence of that. *This interpretation may not be as valid as it first appears, however.* In fact, three points come up against it. 1. Mediterraneans and Africans in whom the endemic form of Kaposi's sarcoma appear *do not* have, for the most part, *any* objective sign of a T-cell immune deficiency. 2. Kaposi's sarcoma on the *skin* of individuals infected by HTLV-III/LAV appear, for most, early in the course of the infection, at a stage when immune deficiency is either *moderate* or *nonexistent*. 3. In general, similarities between two situations is by no means sufficient in establishing their identity: the processes leading to an immuno-deficiency state in AIDS, a consequence of an infection to a retrovirus, are likely to differ from those occurring as a consequence of a medication.

These points lead to the following argument: Kaposi's sarcoma in HTLV-III/LAV infections might not be a mere sequalae of immune deficiency. Another explanation would be required. One such proposes that there is a positive association between the activity of HTLV-III/LAV infected T4-cells and endothelial cells infected by CMV.

New Hypotheses for Kaposi's Sarcoma

T4-lymphocytes are known to produce certain hormonelike substances, the so-called lymphokines. Among these, one or several normally help the growth and multiplication of endothelial cells.

Although not characterized as yet, such factors can be operationally called *endothelial cell growth factors* (End.C.G.F.). In the "normal" situation—ie, in the absence of HTLV-III/LAV—End.C.G.F. would participate in the maintenance of capillaries in areas of the organism where T-lymphocytes are plenty: in lymph nodes, for instance. In certain diseases or in experimental conditions where T4-cells are highly stimulated, more End.C.G.F. is produced and new capillaries develop in the lymph nodes. We are one step toward Kaposi's sarcoma: proliferation of endothelial cells, those cells that normally line up capillaries. HTLV-III/LAV precisely infect those types of lymphocytes that normally releases End.C.G.F. So we are led to the speculation that HTLV-III/LAV might induce secretion of abnormal quantities of End. C.G.F. Schematically, there would be two ways by which this could occur: 1. T4-lymphocytes *in contact* with some constituents of HTLV-III/LAV would be turned on to release lymphokines. One such viral constituent might be the *envelope* of the virus, which appears at the surface of T4-lymphocytes infected by HTLV-III/LAV. 2. T4-lymphocytes, when infected by such a retrovirus, might be turned on *from within* to secrete high amounts of lymphokines. Indeed, retroviruses are well made to induce alterations within the cell machinery.

Now, the growth of endothelial cell in response to the speculative End.C.G.F. would in turn support the growth and multiplication of the cytomegalic virus. Indeed, it is known that endothelial cells growing in cultures produce CMV particles in proportion to their own reproduction. Hence we would have circumscribed the conditions that favor Kaposi's sarcoma secondary to an infection by HTLV-III/LAV without resorting to a mechanism of T-lymphocyte deficiency: HTLV-III/LAV + T4 cells + End.C.G.F. + endothelial cells + CMV = Kaposi.

PREVALENCE OF KAPOSI'S SARCOMA IN HOMOSEXUALS: ANTI-CMV T4-CELLS AS PRIMARY TARGETS FOR HTLV-III/LAV Before infection by HTLV-III/LAV, because of the repeated solicitations which the many times reintroduced CMV represents, certain homosexuals will have developed high numbers of anti-CMV immune cells (T4-lymphocytes specifically reactive against CMV structures). Then occurs the infection by the AIDS retrovirus. Like all retroviruses, it profits from the multiplication of its target cell, both to insert into its chromosomes and replicate within it. Here the targets are T4-lymphocytes, and those reacting to CMV structures are likely to be both numerous and solicitated. The T4 anti-CMV lymphocytes would thus be ideal hosts for HTLV-III/LAV. Being anti-CMV, these T4-cells will anchor themselves to the CMV structures which appear on the surface of endothelial cells harboring CMV. In the close proximity of T4-cells secreting high amounts of End. C.G.F., the CMV-infected endothelial cells will multiply: Kaposi's sarcoma.

KAPOSI'S SARCOMA AND GENETIC CONSTITUTION   All homosexuals having frequent CMV infection do not have Kaposi's sarcoma when they become also infected by HTLV-III/LAV. Indeed, among AIDS cases affecting male homosexuals, not more than 30 percent present with Kaposi on their skin and/or lymph nodes. Others factors must intervene, one among which might be constitutional. According to the preceding construction numerous anti–CMV T4-cells would develop only in certain individuals. Those who express the specimen number 5 of the so-called "Dr" molecules on the surface of their endothelial cells. The Dr-5 is one among a series of molecules which participate in "presenting" the CMV structures to the T4-cells. These molecules are simply inherited from both parents. The individuals expressing the Dr-5 molecules appear more prone to Kaposi's sarcoma than those expressing Dr-1, Dr-2, Dr-3, etc. Thus, the conjunction of six elements might favor the development of Kaposi's sarcoma: HTLV-III/LAV infection + T4-cells + End. C.G.F. + endothelial cells *expressing Dr-5* + CMV.

KAPOSI'S SARCOMA FROM IMMUNO-SUPPRESSIVE DRUGS These medications, if they indeed perturb T-cell functions preferentially, affect T8-cells and not so much T4-cells. Now T8-cells are highly implicated in the control of the multiplicative impulses of the cytomegalovirus. The release of the anti-CMV brake (T8-cells) under the effect of those drugs leads to an intense viral multiplication and to an increase in the quantity of viral structures at the surface of infected (endothelial) cells. Anti–CMV T4-cells become solicitated and multiply upon End. C.G.F., secreted in larger quantities, participates in the development of Kaposi's sarcoma. *Classical Kaposi's sarcoma* in Mediterraneans and Africans might just be a natural geographic variant of the preceding schema. Infection from CMV might indeed be more frequent or more massive in certain areas of the world.

According to the preceding speculations, Kaposi's sarcoma would not necessarily be a sign of serious immune deficiency. It could indicate that T4-cells are being actively stimulated by the retrovirus. This model accommodates the fact that HTLV-III/LAV infections do result in disseminated Kaposi's sarcoma without always causing secondary infections from opportunistic infections.

Secondary Infections from Opportunistic Germs

Certain microbes, not just any (it is wrong to say that AIDS patients catch "just any disease"), will multiply abundantly when the numbers of functioning T4-lymphocytes are reduced in the proportion of some 90 percent. These opportunistic microbes are so-called intracellular because they multiply better inside the cells than outside them, in the blood for instance.

The T4-Lymphocytes, Predators of Intracellular Microbes?

The T4-lymphocytes do not have the chemical equipment necessary to kill microbes. Moreover, these parasites are not concerned with the lymphocytes but with other cells (macrophages, for instance).

By their secretions, the T4-lymphocytes will help the infected cells to resist. The example of the macrophages is demonstrative: one of the factors normally produced by the stimulated T4-lymphocytes is gamma interferon. This factor effectively "activates" the macrophages in their bactericidal function. At the same time, it interferes with the multiplication of certain viruses parasitical on various cells. This molecule has become rare in AIDS patients, and the germs take advantage of this lack.

The infection appears as a symptom (pulmonary infection, digestive infection) when the microbic mass is such that the products secreted by it or by the infected cells become distressing (coughing, breathlessness, diarrhea). The fever is not different, whether it is due to a secondary infection or to that from the AIDS virus. But temperatures up to 40°C with chills are not characteristic of infection by the retrovirus itself.

Secondary infections are thus indirectly linked to failures of the T4-cells, which can no longer "supply" enough biological materials that habitually support all kinds of cells confronting the microbes of intracellular ecology.

Malignant Tumors Complicating AIDS

In a small number of patients, malignant lymphomas have developed. These are cancerous tumors whose original cell belongs to the lymphocyte family (B-lymphocytes). These B-lymphocyte tumors were known before AIDS as they occur relatively frequently in China and Africa (a British surgeon, Dr. Burkitt, had given his name to its description). *Burkitt's lymphomas* in children are numerous in Zaïre and more generally so in the humid regions of equatorial Africa, where another virus is highly endemic and transmitted to children early in their life: the Epstein Barr virus.* E.B. virus infection of

---

*The Epstein Barr virus is a widespread, ubiquitous virus: some 80 percent of European adults carry E.B. Virus in their B-lymphocytes. It rarely causes perceptible disease (infectious mononucleosis); rather, it remains latent, but permanent, in most carriers.

B-lymphocytes, akin to CMV infection of endothelial cells, could promote cancerous events within so parasitized B-cells. Also T-lymphocytes participate in the multiplication of EBV within B-cells. Thus immuno-suppression either from drugs prescribed to prevent a transplant rejection or from a severe HTLV-III/LAV infection of T4-cells favors the occurence of such lymphomas. Also it is possible that some B-cell growth factor(s) could participate. Indeed, HTLV-III/LAV infection of T4-cells brings about a high degree of activation in B-lymphocytes. Thus Burkitt's lymphoma would arise in a combination of factors: HTLV-III/LAV infection of T4-cells, secretion of B-C.G.F.(s), infection of B-lymphocytes by E.B. virus.

Unexplained Symptoms

Initial diarrhea: though not always observed, it seems relatively frequent in Haiti and in Africa. We are unable to say anything about it except that it is not lasting and that it is not linked to the *site* of the initial viral inoculation.

Nonspecific cutaneous lesions: particularly frequent (over 50 percent of the cases) in Haiti. We have no clear indication as to their signification. One fact, however, is worth mentioning: the HTLV virus has, in its composition, a constituent part identical to that of a cellular constituent. This constituent occurs in certain skin cells. "Antivirus" antibodies, recognizing these analogous structures, could make their way into the skin and cause the observed phenomena.

Intolerance of sulfa drugs: nearly 60 percent of the patients who have received a pharmaceutical combination of sulfamide and antibiotic have experienced reactions of fever, eruption, or diminution of white corpuscles. The frequency of these intolerance-reactions excludes a coincidence.

IMMUNOLOGICAL INFECTIONS AND ANOMALIES OBSERVED IN HOMOSEXUALS

"Tropical" Intestinal Infections

MONSIEUR V., BEFORE PRESENTING THE FIRST SYMPTOMS OF INfection from the AIDS virus, had received treatment for amoebas found in his stool and responsible for his diarrhea. These amoebas are frequent in certain tropical regions; intestinal giardia is also a non-aggressive parasite in these regions.

Such tropical diseases are increasingly frequent in homosexuals as a result of certain sexual practices and "exotic" encounters with natives or tourists traveling in tropical regions; this collection of benign infections translates the risk of being contaminated by various microbes, in proportion to the number of the subject's intimate partners. In New York City, 30 to 80 percent of the homosexual population are carriers of amoebas (healthy carriers, for the majority). Aside from the "exotic" label, which certainly sticks to the homosexual population when perceived from the microbic point of view—we may say, semi-officially, that Manhattan is on the way to becoming a tropical island—is this intestinal parasitism susceptible of favoring infection from the AIDS virus? Unless they involve a weakening of the rectal mucous membrane, thus making it more vulnerable, mechanically, such infections remain, in the West, superficial and involve the immune system only slightly. There exists no objective biological reason to suppose that they favor AIDS. The same is true for veneral diseases (including genital herpes, for which there is no positive reason to suppose that it results from an immune deficiency in anyone in particular), and perhaps for hepatitis B as well. These infections are frequent in homosexuals, evidence of the multiplicity of their partners. But they are neither necessary nor sufficient for contamination by the AIDS virus. Not necessary, since observations of AIDS exist without previous infections from these viruses or microbes. Not sufficient, obviously, since the minimal condition required to contract AIDS is to be contaminated by the AIDS virus.

Superficial Lymph Node Swelling in Homosexuals

The number of homosexuals presenting palpable superficial lymph nodes in the neck, armpits, and groin is apparently quite high (over 10 percent of the population?). A proportion of these, difficult to calculate for want of non-ambiguous objective data, are *not* infected by HTLV-III/LAV, but by other viruses frequent in this population: cytomegalic virus, adenovirus, herpes virus. Nor must we omit the relative frequency of syphilitic infections which can involve adenopathies of the same type (secondary syphilis).

These infections or chronic reinfections give rise to a set of immunological modifications analogous to those which are caused by infection from HTLV-III/LAV: dimunution of the number of T4-cells in relation to that of T8-cells; increase of immuno-globulins; transitory cutaneous anergy; alpha interferon in the blood; increase of neopterine excretion.

Biopsy of the node shows the same modifications as those caused by the retrovirus, whose signification they share: solicitation of the immune cells by an alien viral agent and preferential "engagement" of T8-cells in relation to T4-cells in the node and, by reflection, in the blood.

Might not these non-AIDS infections bring with them in principle the cohort of general symptoms which can mark infection by HTLV-III/LAV (undulant fever, night sweats, weight loss)? These symptoms are not specific to infection from the AIDS virus. They are accounted for by the intervention of natural substances produced when the immune system experiences generalized "solicitations." Viruses other than that of AIDS might give rise to analogous symptoms since they "engage" and "solicit" the immune system. Henceforth, with these symptoms, it is impossible to affirm an infection by the retrovirus in a homosexual man presenting with adenopathies. Elsewhere, we know from observation that 90 to 95 percent of the patients will see their swollen lymph nodes disappear in six months, a year, two, even three years. Knowing that 90 to 95 percent of these patients will never have the serious immune deficiency that infection from the retrovirus *sometimes* causes, it is medically inadmissible to terrorize 90 to 95 percent of the individuals by what will turn out to be the phantasm of AIDS, informing them that "they have *the* virus" and that "they will have AIDS."

Immunological Anomalies of Healthy Homosexuals

In the absence of any palpable nodes and of any perceptible disease, "passive" homosexuals have immunological signs subsequent to immune solicitations, comparable in their qualities to those of patients having swollen superficial nodes: lowering of the T4/T8 ratio, increase in the number of lymphocytes in the blood. The interpretation of these anomalies is simple, if we refer, on the one hand, to the presence of various viruses in the sperm of homosexuals having many partners, and, on the other hand, to the "immuno-stimulant" effect of infections from certain viruses, such as the cytomegalic virus. These anomalies, indicative of a state of immune stimulation, are not the sign of a mysterious "pre-AIDS state." But can we exclude that *immune stimulation* might be a factor favoring the infective capacities of the AIDS virus? In terms of cellular biology, might lymphocyte stimulation, before the introduction of the retrovirus into an organism, favor the virus's "infectivity," by placing the T4-cells in a phase of the cellular cycle propitious to the virus's penetration? The retroviruses, in order to "spread" in an organism, infecting first one cell, then others, must "profit" from the cell-multiplication itself. In cell culture *in vitro*, we must stimulate the lymphocytes of an AIDS virus carrier for them to produce retrovirus particles in quantity. This artificial observation is not directly transposable into a complete organism. But it underlines the role of previous or simultaneous lymphocyte stimulation as a factor of virus multiplication.

Another question to raise: What is there in common between the lymphocytes of an infant and those of a homosexual? The lymphocytes at birth and in the first years of life are vigorously stimulated by a multitude of substances supplied by feeding, by the ambient air, by applications to the skin of soaps, perfumes, dyes, and clothing textures. This host of substances "alien" to the infant's lymphocytes. The lymphocytes are thus in full expansion: from infants to homophiles, from drug addicts to hemophiliacs, all are subject to intense immune solicitations, with an immune system in full effervescence. If a retrovirus is introduced, this is the occasion for it to multiply. Would not this mean, *a contrario*, that a little-solicited immune system, an immune system "at peace" or even "exhausted," would be far away from what the AIDS-virus is looking for? Perhaps.

Numerous medical and paramedical staffs in the last four years have been in contact with contaminated biological specimens (blood) and patients with AIDS. No case of AIDS has been reported among these staffs. Now, anyone who frequently handles syringes and needles *pricks* himself, herself. A certain number of nurses have thus been superficially wounded by materials containing the infected cells. The absence of AIDS, despite such inoculations, suggests that a particular immune condition may favor the *infectivity* of the AIDS virus.

Elsewhere, patients in a state of advanced renal insufficiency must resort, in order to survive, to periodic hemodialysis. More than 10,000 patients thus regularly make use of an artificial kidney. And more than 100,000 throughout the world. The incidence of homosexuality in the whole of the male populations being generally constant, it is sociologically unlikely that there is no homosexual in hemodialysis. Homosexual promiscuity being a risk factor (encountering the AIDS virus), at first we are astonished by, and then we attempt to explain, the absence of AIDS in those resorting to hemodialysis. Now, the state of advanced (or as is said: "terminal") renal insufficiency is regularly accompanied by a certain immune deficiency documented by many indications. These observations are compatible with the following hypothesis: if immuno-stimulation favors susceptibility to infection from the AIDS virus, "true" immune deficiency would, by this construction, be somewhat protective instead.

Bruises and Black-and-Blue Marks, Hemorrhagic Tendency in Homosexuals

Prominent bruises for minor impacts, frequently bleeding gums, nosebleeds, tiny patches of dried blood on the skin, expecially in folds and wrinkles, the armpits, on the pelvis: these are the signs of what is called *purpura*. Purpura is a capillary weakness linked with a profound diminution of platelets. The platelets, tiny blood cells, line the capillaries. In the absence of a sufficient number of platelets (less than 10,000 per microliter), the capillaries "burst," spontaneously or under the effect of minor traumatisms. These "thrombopenic purpuras"* have been known for over a century in the West and therefore have no direct links with HTLV-III/LAV. Dozens of observations of this disease, not exceptional in non-homosexuals, have recently

---

Thrombo: platelets; *penia:* lack.

been recorded in the United States in young homosexuals. Since it is certain that thrombopenic purpura is *not* directly linked to the AIDS virus, why this relationship? On the one hand, because this disease seems more frequent in New York City today, coinciding with the multiplication of AIDS cases; on the other, because thrombopenic purpura is linked to infections from various viruses.

The mechanisms by which any viruses might lead to accelerated platelet destruction are not direct: for most viruses involved, thrombopenic purpuras are not due to their infecting the platelets themselves but rather to some "auto-immune" mechanism. Whatever, thrombopenic purpuras can be a manifestation of an HTLV-III/LAV infection. As such, however, it is no more predictive of a future AIDS state than are minor symptoms such as fever, swollen nodes, night sweats. Also, because of its lack of specificity, other viruses must be ruled out before ascribing such thrombopenic purpuras to an infection by the AIDS retro-virus in male homosexuals.

· 7 ·

TREATMENTS AND PROSPECTS

THERE CAN BE NO QUESTION OF FURNISHING AN EXHAUSTIVE IN-
ventory of the treatments undertaken or envisaged, still less of
proposing a practical manual of treatments of AIDS. On the one
hand, the diversity of the situations is too vast. On the other, the
therapeutic efforts now under way cannot yet be assessed, lacking
adequate information. To draw up, today, a list of recognized,
therapeutic practices would be equivalent to considering the problems solved, the repertoire of available treatments complete, or the
therapeutic impasses definitive. This chapter will consider only the
general principles that govern the treatments already used or envisaged before the discovery of the causative virus. Nevertheless, to
treat AIDS today consists mostly in the *consequences* of infection
from the retrovirus rather than the viral infection itself. However, a
series of drugs are now being tried that more directly impeech the
multiplication of the retrovirus.

Disseminated Kaposi's Sarcoma

Cancerous or not, the lesions of Kaposi's sarcoma resemble cancer
on one point: the cells constituting the lesions are in multiplication.
The therapeutic procedures proposed all tend to limit or to halt

these multiplications: chemotherapies, superficial radiation therapy, alpha interferons.

Chemotherapies resort to anti-mitotic substances which oppose mitoses, *i.e.*, cellular multiplication. Their disadvantages are in certain disagreeable secondary effects (nausea, loss of hair, diminution of the quantity of white blood cells) or, in the context of AIDS, unacceptable because of aggravation of immune deficiency. Certain anti-mitotics, effective against the lesions of Kaposi's sarcoma, have no immuno-suppressor effects. Extracts of plants, such as podophyllin and its derivatives, extracts of periwinkle, are effective against Kaposian lesions. Other chemotherapeutic combinations have also been used. The total rate of positive responses, with one or the other of these combinations, varies from 50 to 80 percent.

Superficial radiation therapy or mini-surgery (direct ablation of some lesions) can be proposed, when the lesions are limited in number.

Alpha interferons, in high doses, have been and are being used where they are available. Their effectiveness is real, especially when the patient being treated does not have a high rate of endogenous interferons in his blood. Whatever their modes of action, it is certain that alpha interferons do not favorably modify the tests of immune deficiency in the patients. The results obtained are not better than those of simple or multiple chemotherapies. The secondary effects of this product are not negligible. Considering, as well, the present cost of these treatments, the elements do not add up to make alpha interferon the "miracle drug" of all Kaposi's sarcomas compared to the results of chemotherapies.

Should All Kaposi's Sarcoma Cases Be Treated?

The treatments proposed for Kaposi's sarcoma aim only at effacing or limiting the extension of aesthetically disturbing lesions, occasionally dangerous because affecting important organs such as the lungs, heart, or liver. All Kaposi's sarcoma lesions do not assume disturbing or aggressive aspects. Further, the natural development of such lesions is not necessarily progressive in every case. Since the treatments undertaken do not aim at annihilating the AIDS virus, their use may not be always indicated.

Secondary Infections

The major known risk of infection by HTLV-III/LAV is AIDS itself, *i.e.*, the profound immune deficiency whose consequences are above all infectious: secondary infections from "opportunistic" intracellular germs.

Not all secondary infections are equally serious. Infections from cytomeglaic viruses produce few symptoms and few threatening localizations. On the other hand, cerebral infection from toxoplasmas or pneumocystic pneumonias are immediately dangerous. Antibiotic treatments appropriate for each of the microbes are utilized "on demand," as a consequence of the necessities. But the experience of the last five years has taught us that the symptoms of patent secondary infections are belated, as are concurrently, the applications of antibiotic treatment "on demand." These delays in part explain the failures of anti-microbic treatments. We must therefore try to discover as soon as possible the clinical or biological signs of those secondary infections that we know may have distressing consequences: pneumocystis carinii, toxoplasma, cryptosporidium, atypical tubercle bacilli. We also envisage resorting to systematic prophylactic or preventive treatments, administered even before a discoverable infection. But this apparently logical attitude does not fail to raise certain problems. Medicational intolerances seem to be frequent in patients, and blind antibiotic treatments may be of no real use.

Immune Deficiency

Immune deficiency presently is the most disturbing result of the infection by HTLV-III/LAV. We do not yet know whether the virus directly inflicts or indirectly induces the anomalies in the T4-lymphocytes leading to immune deficiency. But we can regroup, in a strategic perspective, the elements we know we must combat. The process which leads to the state of serious immune deficiency is a process of destruction and of "non-regeneration" of aging T4-cells (lymphoycte aplasia and lymphatic involution). This process is a gradual one and it becomes preoccupying when the T4-cell populations have been *massively* affected. Being unable to "affect" the virus itself, opposing immune deficiency means attempting to palliate or compensate for the destructive or aregenerative process by counting on the apparent slowness of the natural disease, and by anticipating that an advantage, even a modest one, can gain some points against mortality.

What weapons do we possess as of today? *Medications with immuno-stimulant effects:* this generic term includes various substances. They have various poles of action on different cells (lymphocytes or macrophages). They act as elements capable of "soliciting" the immune system. *Hormones* (or thymus extracts): there exist several of these, irregularly available. They may have a positive maturation effect on the reserves of cell strains engendering the T4 daughter-cells. Certain of these substances would have the merit, in certain cases, of being able to mobilize these "reserves" not engaged or paralyzed by the virus. *Replacement cells:* since there is a lack of T-cells, the idea of a substitution for the lacking cells by contributions of lymphocyte cells from some one else has developed. Given the mass of cells produced daily, simple transfusions could not suffice and therefore bone marrow transplants, since bone marrow is rich in cell strains, have been attempted. *Replacement lymphokines:* since the lack of T-cells ultimately leads to a lack of the substances normally produced by T-cells, recourse to massive injections of lymphokines was conceivable, as is successfully practiced in the case of insulin for certain diabetics. Attempts to use gamma interferons and interleukine II* are also under way.

It is too soon to offer definitive judgments as to the effectiveness of these various undertakings. The premises on which they rest are certainly arguable. Immuno-stimulants? But we have seen to what point the immune system was naturally solicited, from the start of the infection. Hormones or thymic factors? But they have not so often given tangible proofs of their effects on human T-cell generation. These theoretical comments yield, in the present circumstances, to the necessity of the undertaking. In this phase, enlightened empiricism must remain the guide of therapeutic attempts.

In any case, a general consideration of the therapeutic projects reveals their deliberately *palliative* and not *curative* nature. Palliative treatments have, in medicine, broad applications and not negligible successes. And they will be all the better adapted when we are able to understand the effects of the virus on the target cells, starting from observations made on patients, and pursued with the analysis of cells in cytocultures in the laboratories.

To eradicate or neutralize the AIDS virus has become the order of the day. The AIDS virus has been identified. Multiple isolates of it have been obtained from cells from American and French patients. These viruses are being analyzed in their structures. Simultaneously studies are under way on the effects the virus exerts upon lymphocytes *in culture*. The model of the feline leukemia virus, whose effects on the cat's lymphocytes *in vivo* are similar to those of the human virus, should lead to profitable information and analogies. Research in this domain should make rapid strides. The time such procedures will take before they can produce appreciable clinical results must be calculated in terms of several years, at least. In the interval, the battle on the terrains where medicine fights when it cannot yet cure must be continued: treatment of symptoms and, quite particularly, here, treatment of secondary infections. However the key and only practical word for the coming years will remain *Prevention*.

---

*Interleukin II is another name for T-cell growth factor, a lymphokine normally secreted by T4-lymphocytes.

$$\cdot 8 \cdot$$

HOW NOT TO CATCH HTLV-III/LAV

Cells and Virus Carriers

HOW DOES SOMEONE GET INFECTED BY THE AIDS VIRUS? AT THE minimum, by exposing him/herself to the contaminated secretions of a virus carrier.

FROM THE VIEWPOINT OF THE VIRUS CARRIER

HTLV-AIDS (HTLV-III/LAV) like leukemia (HTLV-I) resides mostly in the lymphocytes. How to propagate cells like the lymphocytes toward the outer "world"? Theoretically by the intermediary of one's blood, if one bleeds or if one is a blood donor, or by that of secretions: genital, urinary, digestive (saliva and stool).

THE HTLV-LEUKEMIA MODEL IN JAPAN

Male carriers of HTLV-I regularly contaminate women; women carriers, irregularly, men (see page 35, 36). These observations have been made among heterosexual couples living under the same roof and sharing the usual intimacy, sexual and otherwise, of individuals of both sexes. This asymmetry says a great deal about the contagion of the virus outside of specifically sexual intimacy: it appears as nonexistent. Forks, plates, toothbrushes, bedclothes, glasses, handshakes: the question is settled. No reason to suppose that Japanese wives drink out of their husbands' glass, wash with their husbands' bath-glove, eat with their husbands' fork, while the husbands are forbidden to reciprocate in kind. Daily exchanges should be statistically symmetrical, if not in one couple, at least in the totality of Japanese couples.

IS THE JAPANESE KISS INTRANSITIVE?

Does the Japanese wife expose herself to receiving contaminants from her husband's saliva, but not the converse? The Marx Brothers we have interrogated said yes. All others, no. Conclusion: saliva *should* not a good vector. And the virus is not transmitted by the messages quarreling couples send each other (in both directions).* However, since the retrovirus is found in saliva, it might be that French (but not Japanese?) kiss is a way to contaminate a partner.

IS JAPANESE SEXUALITY A SPECIAL KIND?

No doubt. Each culture has its signs and its traditions. But erotic prints, Samurai films, and the testimony of amateur travelers, not to mention of novels, indicate that on the whole their practices are in the end pathetically similar to our own, except for a few flourishes. Conclusion: men, in general, are 'donors" of intimate secretions to women whom anatomy has thus prepared to "receive." Heterosexual biological asymmetry, seen from the angle of lymphocyte projections, is a fact. We can now "cross-check" this simple information with the data on HTLV-I biology, since that virus is a close relative of the AIDS virus, together with the data on the carrier-cells, the T-lymphocytes.

---

*Japanese couples, according to filmed investigation, quarrel in this fashion. Just like Europeans! Well, they *apostrophize each other!*

THE ROUTE OF SPERM AND OF BLOOD

The T-lymphocytes present in sperm are contaminants, because sperm can be deposited upon a mucous membrane (vagina, rectum, mouth).

FROM THE VIEWPOINT OF THE RECEIVER OF THE CONTAMINATED SECRETIONS

The intravenous trail is, with the information on HTLV-Type I the "royal way," with a contamination rate of 60 percent after blood or cell transfusion. The mucous membrane trail is incalculable but discernible. The contaminated cells must be deposited on a "receptive" mucous membrane: anal, vaginal, or even buccal. Fellation, judging from a few anecdotic observations, seems to be a means of possible contamination. Henceforth, apart from transfusions, the preventive aphorism would be: "Not to contract the AIDS virus means not to expose one's receptive mucous membranes to the secretions of a virus carrier."

Who Is a Virus Carrier?

1. A fraction of subjects of both sexes who have lived during the last five years in tropical regions of Central Africa or in Haiti whether or not they are natives of these regions. Recent surveys (October 1984) in Kinshasa, Zaire, conducted on limited number of people, show antibodies to HTLV-III/LAV in around 10 to 20 percent of individuals so tested.

2. An increasingly sizeable fraction of homosexual men in Western countries (North America and Europe) who have had intimate contacts with virus-carrying men from the United States, Haiti, Africa. The latest partial screenings in gays from San Francisco, New York, London, Copenhagen, and Paris (from individuals consulting in veneral disease

clinics) yielded the following counts: respectively 65, 47, 20, 17, 25 percent gave positive reactions.

3. A majority of hemophilic patients who have received factor VIII–enriched blood fractions. Between 40 and 80 percent have been found antibody-positive. (It is not known, however, whether they all are indeed virus-carriers. They might just have received inactivated viruses through transfusion of these fractions.)

4. Drug addicts of both sexes in the U.S. Alarming figures of over 80 percent have been found among small group of New York drug users.

5. An unsizeable minority of people who would have received HTLV-III/LAV contaminated blood or blood products in the last five years. Maybe as many as 1,000 blood recipients as of December 1984.

In the Absence of Symptoms, Can the Virus-Portage Be Detected?

Since the discovery of HTLV-III/LAV, it has become technically feasible to detect specific antibodies in the serum of people exposed to it. However, it has not been established yet which of the antibody-positive individuals are actual carriers of the infectious form of the virus. In the laboratory, cultures of contaminated lymphocytes from sperm, saliva, lymph node, or blood are considered the only definite way to demonstrate infectious virus in a given person at this time.

AIDS in Tropical Zones

Apart from contamination through blood transfusions, HTLV-III/LAV infections could well be propagated through intimate heterosexual contacts (not withstanding mutual contaminations through male homosexual contacts). Medicinal injections with unsterilized syringes and needles outside or inside hospital settings could play their role in the dissemination of the virus. Transmission through insect bites carrying infected human lymphocytes from one to another individual does not seem to represent a real danger.

AFTERWORD

COMING FROM EQUATORIAL AFRICA, A TROPICAL VIRUS HAS AR-
rived among us, in the United States and in Europe. The rapidity
with which the epidemic has been spreading is attested to by the
following figures.

In the United States, declared cases of AIDS have burst up from
55 (before 1981) to 225 (December 1981), to 832 (December 1982), to
3,308 (January 1984), to over 7,000 in November 1984. In the beginning
of the epidemic the cases doubled every six months. The actual slope
of this curve has been somewhat curbing down since February 1984.
Is the epidemic fading out? Is the retrovirus, after having caused
devastation among the most fragile, on its way out? Viruses of the
HTLV-III/LAV type are not of the evanescent kind. Quite to the
contrary, they are here to stay and propagate. And they have. Every
bit of the latest information on the numbers of those who carry the
virus without suffering from it indicates that it has installed itself
among the exposed populations and is dwelling well: in San Francisco, where some 30 percent of activist gay men have swollen
superficial lymph-nodes, an increasing majority has been shown to
have been exposed to the virus: antibodies to it have been found in
the serum of 1 percent (before 1979), 25 percent (1983), 65 percent

(early 1984), and now 85 percent of them. In New York and New Jersey, 90 percent of IV drug users could be virus carriers.

In Europe, 20 to 30 percent of French, Danish, German, and English homosexuals consulting in V.D. clinics are nonsymptomatic carriers of the virus—it has been established that infections by HTLV-III/LAV are 10 to 100 times more frequent than the "complete" AIDS. Thus, far from disappearing, the once strange virus is no doubt on its way to becoming familiar.

Will the spread continue? Within the already exposed groups, unless major behavioral changes occur expressedly, it should definitely do so. It also has become clear that women harboring the virus may contaminate their partners during sexual intimacy, and so do men to their women contacts. Transfusions of contaminated blood will continue to cause exceptional cases until tests are available that detect virus-carriers efficiently.

Until cure is in proximate sight, until vaccines are produced (three years, ten years?), the only practical masterword against AIDS and its causative virus will remain PREVENTION.

With AIDS we have the feeling we are watching a horror film that is half-reality, half-fiction. The epidemiological scenario plays itself out against a world background. The leading parts—of actors or of spectators—have been cast. It is being staged at home and travel agencies are no longer the only co-producers. Biological laws have at first taken over the direction. Fate might pull the whole thing together, but the cutting and montage is still up to us. With eyes wide, but also wide open, we watch and we know what is happening. Let us make use of this knowledge to decide, if and when possible, to choose what will happen to us.

Dr. J. L.
Paris, October 1984

ACKNOWLEDGMENTS

The author wants to thank all those—physicians, biologists, journalists, ethnologists, sociologists, philosophers, psychoanalysts, and men of letters who have helped him in this enterprise by their information, their criticism and/or their friendship:

J. Allen, J. Curran, P. Drotman, D. Francis, H. Jaffe, D. Kramer (Atlanta); C. Gigase (Antwerp): W. Blattner, R. Gallo, B. Hahn, M. Robert-Guroff, M. Popovic, P. Siram, R. Ting, F. Wong-Staal (Bethesda); M. Koch (Berlin); J. David, M. Essex, E. Kass, S. Schlossman (Boston); N. Clumek, M. Rolland, Y. Sprecher (Brussels); B. Velimerovic (Copenhagen); R. Penny (Darlinghurst); C. Kirkpartick (Denver); B. Haynes (Durham); M. C. Foulon, M. V. Jubert, D. Mathez, M. Nourry, J. Patard, P. Prunet, F. Thorez, M. Tulliez (Garches); G. Y. Causse (Geneva); H. de Diettrich, K. Lennert, P. Racz (Hamburg and Kiel); D. Fuchs, G. Reibnegger, H. Wachter (Innsbruck); K. Bila, M. Paku (Kinshasa); I. Miyoshi (Kochi); D. Stehelin (Lille); R. G. Catovsky, N. Galbraith, M. Greaves, D. Jeffries, J. Hutt (London); A. Berthoux, P. Poirot, C.B. de Thee, J. L. Touraine (Lyon-Saint-Etienne); K. Okochi (Maīdashi); G. Giraldo (Naples).

C. Bo Dupont, N. Fain, A. Friedman-Kein, L. Kramer, L. Laubenstein, J. Lawrence, L. Mass, C. Metroaka, C. Nathan, A. Rubinstein, B. Safai, J. Tomba, E. White, D. Williams, A. Zolla-Pazner (New York).

J. Acar, M. A. d'Adler, P. Amstutz, G. Barbedette, F. Barre-Sinoussi, E. Bouvet, P. Bronstein, J. C. Brouet, J. B. Brunet, P. Burian, M. Capelier, P. Catalan, I. Caubarrère, E. Chasny, J. C. Chermann, E. Conan, A. Coutinho, M. Devergh, J. Deschamps, C. Diaz, M. Dourane, P. Druet. J.-P. Escande, P.

Acknowledgments

Even, B. Frank, A. Fribourg-Blanc, S. Gisselbrecht, J. Guir, J. Hewitt, J. C. Kadouche, B. Kouchner, C. Lejeune, J. P. Levey, C. Mayaud, B. Messing, J. L. Montagueier, J. Mousallier, T. Nebout, P. Nochy, R. Offenstadt, M. Pathamavong, M. F. Pisier, P. Poussier, P. Pullick, D. Quessada, M. F. Ricard Girod Daguet, F. Reyes, G. Saimot, M. Szafran, I. Sezary, A. Sicard, M. Theodori, A. Venet, J. P. Vernant, J. C. Weil, D. Zagury (Paris).

J. E. Rohde (Port-au-Prince); M. Conant (San Francisco); J. P. Vernant (Sèvres).

BIBLIOGRAPHY

Medical journals have abundantly reported information pertinent to AIDS and its virus, a fraction of which can be found in the following articles:

ANNALS OF INTERNAL MEDICINE

1982. FRIEDMAN-KIEN, A.F.; LAUBENSTEIN, L.J.; et al. "Disseminated Kaposi's Sarcoma in Homosexual Men." Vol. 96: pp. 693–97.
1983. DAVIS, K., HORSBURGH, C.; et al. "Acquired Immunodeficiency Syndrome in a Patient with Hemophilia." Vol. 98: pp. 284–96.
PICHENIK, A.; FISCHL, M.; et al. "Opportunistic Infections and Kaposi's Sarcoma among Haitians: Evidence of a New Acquired Immunodeficiency State." Vol. 98: pp. 277–84.
JAFFE, H.W.; KEEWHAN, CHOI; et al. "National Case-Control Study of Kaposi's Sarcoma and Pneumocystis Carinii Pneumonia in Homosexual Men: Part I, "Epidemiologic Results." Vol. 99: pp. 145–51.

BLOOD

1982. GALLO, R.C., and WONG-STAAL, F. "Retrovirus as Etiologic Agents of Some Animal and Human Leukemias and as Tools of Elucidation the Molecular Mechanism of Leukemogenesis." Vol. 60: pp. 545–57.

IMMUNOLOGY TODAY

1982. SHEARER, G., and HURTENBACH, U. "Is Sperm Immunosuppressive in Male Homosexuals and Vasectomized Men?" Vol. 3: pp. 153–54.

Bibliography

INTERNATIONAL JOURNAL OF CANCER

1983. HUNSMANN, G.; SCHNEIDER, J.; et al. "Detection of Serum Antibodies to Adult T-Cell Leukemia Virus in Non-Human Primates and in People from Africa." Vol. 32: pp. 329–32.
1984. MAEDA, Y.; FURUKAWA, M.; et al. "Prevalence of Possible Adult T-Cell Leukemia Virus-Carries among Volunteer Blood Donors in Japan: a Nation-wide Study." Vol. 33: pp. 717–20.

JOURNAL OF THE NATIONAL CANCER INSTITUTE

1971. ANDERSON, L.; JARRETT, J.; et al. "Feline Leukemia Virus Infection of Kittens. Morbility Associated with Atrophy of the Thymus and Lymphoid Depletion." Vol. 47: pp. 807–17.

LANCET

1981. THOMSEN, H.K.; JACOBSEN, M.; et al. "Kaposi Sarcoma among Homosexual Men in Europe." Vol. ii: p. 688.
1982. MAURICE, P.D.L.; SMITH, N.P.; et al. Kaposi's Sarcoma with Benign Course in a Homosexual." Vol. i: p. 571.
MARMOR, M.; LAUBENSTEIN, L.; et al. "Risk Factors for Kaposi's Sarcoma in Homosexual Men." Vol. i: pp. 1084–87.
1983. KOMURO, A.; HAYAMI, M.; et al. "Vertical Transmission of Adult T-Cell Leukaemia Virus." Vol. i: p. 240.
YAMAMOTO, N.; HINUMA, Y.; et al. "Africa Green Monkeys Are Infected with Adult T-Cell Leukaemia Virus or a Closely Related Agent." Vol. i: pp. 240–41.
MIYOSHI, I.; FUJISHITA, M.; et al. "Horizontal Transmission of Adult T-Cell Leukemia Virus from Male to Female Japanese Monkey." Vol. i: p. 241.
BYGBJERG, J.C. "AIDS in a Danish Surgeon." Vol. i: p. 925.
St. JOHN, R.K. "AIDS and Africa Swine Fever." Vol. i: p. 1335.
DARROW, W., et al. "Passive Anal Intercourse as a Risk Factor for AIDS in Homosexual Men." Vol. ii: p. 160.
MIYOSHI, I., et al. "ATLV in Japanese Patient with AIDS." Vol. ii: p. 275.
WALKER, D.A., and LILLEYMAN, J.S. "Pseudo-AIDS." Vol. ii: p. 345.
GRECO, R. "Haiti and the Stigma of AIDS." Vol. ii: pp. 515–16.

BIBLIOGRAPHY

BRUNET, J.B.; BOUVET E.; et al. "Acquired Immunodeficiency Syndrome in France." Vol. ii: pp. 700–01.

TAGUCHI, H.; FUJISHITA, M.; et al. "HTLV Antibody Positivity and Incidence of T-Cell Leukemia ATL in Kochi Perfecture, Japan." Vol. ii: p. 1029.

KAUFMANN, C.; WEINBERGER, D.; et al. "AIDS in 1959?" Vol. ii: pp. 1136–37.

1984. FLEMING, A.F. "HTLV from Africa to Japan." Vol. i: p. 279.

DOWNING, R.G.; EGIN, R.P.; et al. "African Kaposi's Sarcoma and AIDS." Vol. i: pp. 478–80.

MATHUR WAGH, U.; SPIGLAND, I.; et al. "Longitudinal Study of Persistent Generalised Lymphadenopathy in Homosexual Men: Relation to Acquired Immunodeficiency Syndrome." Vol. i: pp. 1033–38.

BRUN VESINET, F.; BARRE SINOUSSI, F.; et al. "Detection of IgG Antibodies to Lymphadenopathy Associated Virus in Patients with AIDS or Lymphadenopathy Syndrome." Vol. i: pp. 1253–56.

BAYLEY, A.C. "Aggressive Kaposi's Sarcoma in Zambia, 1983." Vol. i: pp. 1318–20.

SAFAI, B.; GROOPMAN, J.E.; et al. "Seroepidemiological Studies of Human T-Lymphotropic Retrovirus Type III in AIDS." Vol. i: pp. 1438–40.

VAN DE PERRE, P.; LEPAGE, P.; et al. "Acquired Immunodeficiency Syndrome in Rwanda." Vol. ii: pp. 62–65.

PIOT, P.; TAELMAN, H.; et al. "Acquired Immunodeficiency Syndrome in a Heterosexual Population in Zaire." Vol. ii: pp. 65–69.

MATHEZ, D.; LEIBOWITCH, J.; et al. "Antibodies to HTLV-III Associated Antigens in Populations Exposed to AIDS Virus in France." Vol. ii: p. 460.

POPOVIC, M.; SARNGADHARAN, M.G.; READ, E.; et al. "Detection, Isolation and Continuous Production of Cytopathic Retroviruses (HTLV-III) from Patients with AIDS and Pre-AIDS." *Science.* 1984. 224 : 497–500.

ARYA, S.K.; GALLO, R.C.; HAHN B.H.; et al. "Homology of Genome of AIDS Associated Virus with Genomes of Human T-Cell Leukemia Viruses." *Science.* 1984. (in press).

MORBIDITY AND MORTALITY WEEKLY REPORT

1982. Center for Disease Control. "A Cluster of Kaposi's Sarcoma and Pneumocystis Carinii among Homosexual Male Residents of Los Angeles and Orange Counties, California." Vol. 32: pp. 305–07.

Bibliography

Epidemiologic notes and reports. "Opportunistic Infections and Kaposi's Sarcoma among Haitians in the United States." Vol. 31: p. 353.

1983.   HARRIS, C.; BUTKUS, M.D.; et al. "Immunodeficiency among Female Sexual Partners of Males with Acquired Immune Deficiency Syndrome (AIDS)." Vol. 31: p. 697.

1984.   DE JARLAIS, D.C.; MARMOR, M.; et al. "Antibodies to a Retrovirus Etiologically Associated with Acquired Immunodeficiency Syndrome (AIDS) in Populations with Increased Incidences of the Syndrome." Vol. 33: pp. 377–79.

McCLURE, H.; SWENSON, B.; et al. "Experimental Infection of Chimpanzees with Lymphadenopathy-Associated Virus." Vol. 33: pp. 442–43.

NATURE

1984.   BUDIANSKY, S. "Problems of New Blood Test." Vol. 309: p. 106.

NEW ENGLAND JOURNAL OF MEDICINE

1983.   JONCAS, J.; DELAGE, G.; et al. "Acquired (or Congenital) Immunodeficiency Syndrome in Infants Born of Haitian Mothers." Vol. 308: p. 842.

CURRAN, J.W. "AIDS: Two Years Later." Vol. 309: pp. 609–11.

CINEAS, F. "Haitian Ambassador Deplores AIDS Connection." Vol. 309: p. 669.

1984.   CURRAN, J.; LAWRENCE, D.; et al. "Acquired Immunodeficiency Syndrome (AIDS) Associated with Transfusions." Vol. 310: pp. 69–75.

SCOTT, G.B.; BUCK, B.H.; et al. "Acquired Immunodeficiency Syndrome in Infants." Vol. 310: pp. 76–81.

JARLAIS, C. DE; MARMOR, M.; et al. "Kaposi's Sarcoma among Four Different AIDS Risk Groups." Vol. 310: p. 1119.

SCIENCE

1983.   BARRE, F.; CHERMANN, J.C.; et al. "Isolation of a T-Lymphotropic Retrovirus from a Patient at Risk for Acquired Immune Deficiency Syndrome (AIDS)." Vol. 220: pp. 868–70.

1984.   MARK, J.L. "Strong New Candidate for AIDS Agent." Vol. 224: pp. 475–77.

GALLO, R.C.; SALAHUDDIN, S.Z.; et al. "Frequent Detection and

Isolation of Cytopathic Retrovirus (HTLV-III) From Patients with AIDS and at Risk of AIDS." Vol. 224: pp. 500–03.

SARNGADHARAN, M.G.; POPOVIC, M.; et al. "Antibodies Reactive with Human T-Lymphotropic Retroviruses (HTLV-III) in the Serum of Patients with AIDS." Vol. 224: pp. 506–08.

VOX SANGUINIS

1984. OKOCHI, K.; SATO, H.; et al. "A Retrospective Study on Transmission of Adult T-Cell Leukemia Virus by Blood Transfusion: Seroconversion in Recipients." Vol. 46: pp. 245–53.

INDEX

A

Acquired Hepato-Deficiency Syndrome (AHDS), 106
Actuel, Paris, 90
Adenopathies, 109
Adenovirus, 141
Africa/African, 18, 36, 38–40, 42, 55, 60, 65–66, 156
  AIDS hypothesis for, 21, 24–25, 68
  HTLV in, 72
  Kaposi's sarcoma in, 23
  swine fever, 69
AHDS, *see* Acquired Hepato-Deficiency Syndrome
AIDS
  African, 21; hypothesis for, 21, 24–25, 68
  anomalies observed in, 96
  appearance of, in America and Europe, 18–19
  babies with, 33
  before 1980, 63
  bisexuality in transmission of, 33, 35
  Caribbean, first cases reported in, 27
  carriers, 33, 50, 117–18; detecting, 86
  Caucasian, 21
  CDC volunteers and, 15
  contagiousness of, 8
  contracted by homosexuals, 6
  dating of, 63
  defining, 16
  diagnosing, 17
  discovered in women, 7
  drug users with, 32, 154
  epidemiology, 20
  Europeans in Africa with, 67
  feline, 44
  first descriptive accounts, 17
  genetic link sought to homosexuality, 96
  geographical distribution, 19–21, 42, 68
  Haitian, 27, 41, 78–79
  hemophiliac(s), 7, 26, 31–32, 63, 67, 81–83, 87, 154
  Hepatitis B, resemblence to, 8
  heterosexual, 38, 62, 78
  history of, 72
  homosexual(s), 6, 8, 31, 37, 69, 95
  in Miami, 69
  incubation periods, 33
  infections characteristic of, 17, 24, 28
  introduction of, in America and Europe, 21, 156
  Japanese cases, 26–27, 60
  medical staffs in contact with, 143
  microbes as agent of, 8
  monogamous cases of, 7
  morbid developments leading to, 104

INDEX

AIDS (con't.)
mothers with, 33
new disease, 16
nonsexual cases, 19
numbers of cases reported, 27, 77, 156
outlining syndrome, 17
Paris study of 1982, 5
post transfusion, 82
prevention, 35, 157
prior symptoms, 107
promiscuity and, 5
prostitutes with, 36
rate of increase, 19, 157
risk groups, 78, 87
rumors, 5
scientific procedure in investigating, 16
symptoms, 101–102, 104, 108;
     nonspecific, 107; unexplained, 139
tests, 117, 119
transmission, 32, 41, 81; bisexual,
     33; through blood, 31–33, 37,
     86; chains of, 7, 35; in Haiti, 41;
     homosexual, 73, 78; by
     injections, 39; interhuman, 57;
     through mucous membrane
     abrasions, 38; through sexual
     contact, 35, 37; by syringes, 39;
     woman-to-man, 36
treatment, 146
tropical disease, 73, 154
tropical sexual genesis, 91
victims, average ages of, 21; types, 32
viral hypothesis, 20
virus, infects special cells, 42;
     distinctive signs of, 60;
     HTLV-III/LAV, 84, 118; carried
     by healthy subjects, 34; trail of,
     120; "lymphophile", 30; specific
     to, 13; tropical, 92
wild speculations about, 20
women with, 35
AIDS-aplasia, 46
AIDS-HTLV, 60, see also
     HTLV-III/LAV
Albumin fractions, 88
Alpha interferons, 91, 125–27, 129–30, 147
American Hospital in Paris, 5
Amoebas, 102, 140

Amyl nitrite, 4, 5
Anemia, lymphocyte, 44
Angola, Africa, 22, 55, 68
Ante/Sperm, 7
Anti-CMV immune cells, 136
Anti-hemophiliac concentrates, 88
Anti-hemophiliac factor, 82
Anti-hepatitis B vaccines, 88
Anti-HTLV antibodies, 58
Antibody testing, 118
Antigens, 122
Antilles, 50
AR-BO viruses, 39
Armour, drug laboratory, 85
Aspergillus fumigatus, 115
Atypical tubercle bacilli, 148
Auto-transfusion, 88

B
B-cell-leukemia, 47
B-cells, 125
B-lymphocyte tumors, 138
B-lymphocytes, 47
Babies with AIDS, 33
Behring, drug laboratory, 85
Beta-2-microglobulin, 125, 127
Biopsies, 119–20, 141
Bisexuality in transmission of AIDS,
     33, 35
Blood, 49, 50, 151, 153
     anti-HTLV antibodies in, 58
     drug addict donors, 86
     homosexual donors, 85
     sources, 64, 85
     synthetic products, 88
     transfusion of contaminated, 86, 105
     transmitting AIDS, 7, 31–32, 37, 81,
     86
Blood cells, transmitting HTLV, 59
Blood donor risk group, 87
Blood products, 81
Bone marrow infections, 115
Brain, toxoplasma in, 17
Brazil, 60
Bucco-esophagial infections, 115
Burkitt's lymphoma, 115, 138,
     139
Burundi, 21, 24

Index

C

Cambridge, MA, 44
Cameroon, 21
Cancer, 131
Candida albicans, 21–22, 103–105, 115, 121–22
Canton, China, 56
Cape Verde Islands, 21, 23
Caribbean, 27, 42, 50, 55, 60
Carrefour, Haiti, 77
Carriers of AIDS, 33–34, 49, 117–18, 151, 153
  detecting, 86
  HTLV, 51, 60; healthy, 60
Cats with AIDS, 44
Caucasians with AIDS, 21, 23
CDC, *see* National Centers for Disease Control
Cells, 48–49
  anti-CMV immune, 136
  blood, transmitting HTLV, 59
  endothelial, 133
  leukemia, 131
  lymphocyte, 45
  replacement, 149
  target, 15
Centers for Disease Control, National (CDC), 8, 15, 23, 27, 77
Cerebral infection, 115, 148
Cerebral toxoplasmosis, 28
Chad, 21
Chemotherapies, 147
Chermann, Dr., 70
Childbirth, HTLV transmission during, 59
Children, AIDS discovered in, 7, 33
China, 53, 56, 91
Chromosomes, 11, 48
Cirrhosis, 106
Claude-Bernard Hospital, Paris, 22
CMV infections, 136–37, 139, *see also* Cytomegalovirus
Cold Spring Harbor, NY, 26
Colombia, 50
Congo-Brazzaville, 21, 65
Contagiousness of AIDS, *see* AIDS, transmission of
Cryprecipitates, lyophilized, 82

Cryptococci, 21, 24
Cryptococcus neoformans, 115
Cryptocosis, 65
Cryptosporidium, 17, 115, 148
Cuba/Cuban(s)
  in Angola, 68
  expel homosexuals, 68
  swine fevers in, 69
Cutaneous anergy, 122–23
Cutaneous lesions, 107, 109, 139
Cutaneous tests, 121–22
Cutter, drug laboratory, 85
Cytoculture, 49, 50, 71, 118, 124
Cytomegalic infections, 115, 133, 141–42
Cytomegalovirus (CMV), 43, 137

D

Dermatitis, serborrheic, 110
Désirade, Island of, 50, 56
Diagnosing AIDS, 16–17, 117, 129
Diarrhea, 107–108, 139
Dias, Bartholomeu, 57
DNA recombinants, 91
Dominica, 27, 50
Drug users, 78, 154
  AIDS discovered in, 7, 32
  blood donor, 86
  risk group, 87
  targeted for opprobrium, 79
Duvalier, Jean-Claude, 80

E

Ebola fever, 66–67
Encephalitis, 115
Endogenous etyomegalovirus, 134
Endogenous microbes, 105
Endopyrogenes, 129–30
Endorphine beta, 130
Endothelial cell growth factors, 133, 135, 139
Enzyme REverse TRranscriptase, 12, 48
Enzymes, 48
Epidemiology Intelligence Service, 77
Epidemiology of AIDS, 20
Epstein-Barr virus, 47, 115, 138
Exotic HTLV, 59

F

Factor VIII, 82–85
Fatigue, 106–108
Federal Food and Drug Administration, 64
Feline leukemia, 44, 49, 59, 150
Fellation, 153
FeLV virus, 45, 49
Feminism, 96
Fever, 108
Fibroscopes, 19
Free Neopterine, 126
French Ministry of Health, 5
Fréquence Gaie (gay radio station), 5
Funai-Oita, Island of Kyushu, 54

G

Gabon, 21
Gai Pied, homosexual newspaper, 94
Gallo, Robert, 70
Gamma globulin, 88
Gamma interferons, 91, 138, 150
Ganglion, 120
Gay Related Immune Deficiency
(GRID), 3, 94
Geographical distribution of AIDS, 19,
20–21
German measles, 126
Giardia, intestinal, 140
Glands, superficial, 109
GRID, (Gay Related Immune
Deficiency). 3, 94
Grippe, 108
Groupe de Travail Français, 70
Guadeloupe, Island of, 56

H

Haiti/Haitian, 7, 38, 62–63, 67, 69
AIDS, in, 41, 79; numbers of cases,
27, 77; since 1975, 78
close hotels, 80;
HTLV in, 55, 60, 71
targeted for opprobrirum, 79
Hakate, Island of Kyushu, 54
Harvard School of Public Health, 44
Hemo-Caribbean and Co., 64
Hemodialysis, 144
Hemophilia/hemophiliac(s), 26, 31–32,
63, 67, 81–83, 87

AIDS among, 7, 82, 154; statistical
date on, 83
risk groups, 87
Hepatic deficiency, 106
Hepatitis B, 34, 39–40, 85–87,
105
frequency of, 9
symptoms, 106
Hepatotropic virus, 118
Herpes, 104–105, 115, 141
Heterosexual AIDS, 38, 62, 78
Hirado, Island of Kyushu, 54
Histoplasma capsulatum, 115
Hodgkin's disease, 131
Homosexual(s)/homosexuality, 6, 8, 31,
35, 37
absent in African hypothesis, 25
HTLV, 59
American, percentage with AIDS,
8, 60, 90
blood donors, 85
contracted AIDS, 6
diseases of, 141
excrete cytomegalis virus in sperm,
133
expelled from Cuba, 68
hemorrhagic tendency in, 144
immune anomalies among, 96, 142
lymph node swelling in, 141
lymphocytes of, 143
Kaposi's sarcoma as disease of, 132
in Miami, 69
promiscuity, 6
passive, 142
risk group, 87
targeted for opprobrium, 79
transmitting AIDS, 32, 37, 73, 78
tropical diseases of, 140
use of poppers, 4
with CMV infection, 136
Hormones, 122, 149
HTLV, 47, 51, 69, 70
African virus, 55, 71
American, 55
cancerization of T4-lymphocytes, 49
carriers, 50–53, 60
geographic distribution, 54–57, 60
Haitian, 71

HTLV *(continued)*
 intrachromosomic, 49
 Japanese, 71, 86
 new virus, 49
 retrovirus, 48
 T-cells infected by, 50
 transmission, during pregnancy, 59;
  during sexual contact, 57;
  mother to child, 58–59
 variant hypothesis confirmed, 87
HTLV-AIDS, *see* HTLV-III/LAV
HTLV-I, 64, 72, 83–84, 88
HTLV-III/LAV, 62, 67, 70, 83–84, 88,
  101, 107–110, 151
 hosts for, 136
 identified as AIDS, 118
 immune deficiency as result of, 149
 infection, 112, 123, 139
 Kaposi's sarcoma as early
  manifestation of, 110
 resembling other diseases, 113
 resides in lymphocytes, 151
 risk of infection by, 148
 symptoms, 104–105
 tests for, 117
Human T-cell Leukemia virus, *see*
 HTLV
Human T-cell Lymphotropic virus, *see*
 HTLV
Human T-Lymphotropic, 72
Hyperplasia-leukemia, 46
Hypertrophied ganglion, 119
Hypertrophied nodes, 109

I

Immune anomalies
 among homosexuals, 96
 pronounced, 104
Immune cells, infection of, 101
Immune deficiency, 134, 149
 degrees of, 116
 symptoms, 101
Immuno, drug laboratory, 85
Immuno-stimulants, 150
Immuno-suppressive drugs, 136
Incubation periods of AIDS, 33
India, 53
Indonesia, 53, 54

Infections, 115
 characterizing AIDS, 17, 24, 28
 from CMV, 137
 intestinal, 140
 lung, 103
 non-AIDS, 142
 opportunistic, 117
 retrovirus, 120
 secondary, 102, 114, 116–17, 121,
  137, 148
 syphilitic, 141
 see also HTLV-III/LAV
Infectious mononucleosis, 47, 126
Injections transmitting AIDS, 39
Insects, 67
Intercellular bacteria, 115
Interferons, 91, 125–27, 129, 130, 138,
  147, 150
Interleukin II, 49, 150
Intestinal giardia, 140
Intestinal infections, 115
Intestines, cryptosporidium in, 17
Intrachromosomic HTLV, 49
Isospora belli, 115
Ivory Coast, 24

J
Jamaica, Island of, 27, 50, 56
Japan/Japanese, 42, 54, 58–59, 86, 151,
  152
 AIDS in, 26–27
 HTLV in, 71
Jaundice, 106
Jesuits, 54

K
Kagoshima, Japan, 54
Kaposi's Sarcoma, 18, 23, 26, 77, 107
 in Africa, 65
 biopsies, 119
 and cytomegalic infections, 133
 definition, 110, 131–32
 disappear after radiation, 112
 and genetic constitution, 136
 in Haiti, 62
 homosexual disease, 132, 135
 immune collapse and, 17
 lesions, 120

Kaposi's Sarcoma (*con't.*)
new hypotheses for, 134
resembling cancer, 146
Kaposi's syndrome, 68, 115
Kenya, 24, 69
Kenya macaques, 68
Kinshasa, Zaire, 38, 65, 67, 153
Kobe-Osaka, Japan, 54
Kochi, Japan, 58, 86
Kyushu, Island of, 54, 60

L
Lamblias, 102
Las Casas, Dr. (missionary priest), 56
Lassa, Nigeria, 66
Lassa virus, 67
Leishmania donovani, 115
Lesions, cutaneous, 109, 110
Leukemia, 26–27, 50, 83
    AIDS and, 45
    B-cell, 47
    cells, 131
    feline, 44, 49, 150
    HTLV, 70
Libido, loss of, 107–108
Liver, 106
London *Lance*, 24
Lung infections, 103
Lung, pneumocystis in, 17
Lymph nodes, 29, 49, 106, 109, 130, 141
    biopsies of, 120, 141
Lymphadenopathies, 109
Lymphadenopathy Associated Virus,
    see HTLV-III/LAV
Lymphatic ganglia, 50
Lymphatic involution, 149
Lymphocyte(s), 22, 28, 31, 37, 45, 59,
    103, 105–106, 117, 122
    anemia, 44
    aplasia, 149
    of category T, 101
    class-B, 125–26
    count, 123
    differential, 123
    functions in cytoculture, 124
    HTLV and, 55
Lymphokines, 122, 125, 149
Lymphomas, malignant, 138

Lymphotropic retrovirus, 101
Lyophilized cryoprecipitates, 82

M
Macrophages, 122, 124, 137, 138
Malaria, 39, 65
Male prostitution, 90
Mali, 21
Malignant tumors, 138
Marburg, West Germany, 66
Marburg virus, 67
Maridi, Africa, 66
Martinique, Island of, 27, 56
Masters and Johnson, 34, 35
Measles, 24
Meningitis, 115
Mental disturbance, 106
Mexico, 60
Miami, FL, 27, 68–69, 80
Microbes
    as likely AIDS agent, 8
    distributions of, 92
    endogenous, 105
Ministry of Health, French, 5
Molecular probes, tracer, 14
Monocyte, 130
Mononucleosis, infectious, 47, 126
Montagnier, Dr., 70
Mothers with AIDS, 33
Mozambique, 22
Mumps virus, 122
Mycobacteria, 115

N
Nagasaki, Japan, 54
National Centers for Disease Control
    (CDC), 23, 27, 77
National Institutes of Health, 77
New England Journal of Medicine, 80
New York City, 27, 79
Newark, NJ, 27
Nicaragua earthquake, 64
Nigeria, 66
Night sweats, 107–108, 142
Nocardia asteriodes, 115
Non-AIDS infections, 142
Nucleic acid, 11, 12, 14, 48, 91, 118
Nzara, Sudan, 66

Index

P
Palace, the (Parisian nightclub), 5
Panama, 56
Papovavirus, 22, 115
Parvo-viruses, 69
Pathology, tropical, 23
Plasma, 64, 84, 85
Plasmaphereses, 64
Plasmodium, 39
Platelets, 82, 84, 144
Pneumocystic pneumonias, 148
Pneumocystis, 12, 19, 92
Pneumocystis carinii, 21–22, 103, 115, 148
Pneumonia, 22, 24, 111, 115
Poppers, 4, 5
Port-au-Prince, Haiti, 63, 69, 77
Pre-AIDS, 107
Pregnancy, HTLV transmission
    during, 59
Prevention of AIDS, 35
Promiscuity, 5–6, 90
Prostitutes with AIDS, 36
Prostitution, male, 90
Protozoa, 115
Pulmonary infections, 115, 138
Purpura, 144
Pyrodermatitis, 110

R
Radiation therapy, superficial, 147
Rectoscopies, 38
Replacement cells, 149
Retinitis, 115
Retrovirus, 12, 33–34, 70–71
    AIDS, 111
    HTLV, 48
    infections by, 120
    lymphotropic, 101
REverse TRanscriptase enzyme, 12, 48
Risk groups, 78, 87
Ruanda, 21, 24

S
Saliva, 37
St. Vincent, Island of, 50
San Francisco, CA, 156

Santo Domingo, 55
Sarcopithes ethiops, 68
Secondary infections, 102, 114, 116–17,
    121, 137, 148
Septicemias, 115
Serborrheic dermatitis, 110
Sex, liberalization of, 90
Sexual contact as transmitter of AIDS, 35
Sezany's Disease, *see* Leukemia
Shikoki, Japan, 51
Skin lesions, 109
Society of Jesus, 54
Sperm, 37, 73, 153
Spleen, 29, 115
St. Barthelemy, Island of, 56
Streptococci, 122
Sudan, 66
Sulfa drugs, intolerance of, 139
Sunda Islands, 54
Superficial ganglis, 107
Superficial glands, 109
Superficial warts, 115
Surinam, 50, 56, 60
Swine fever epidemics, 69
Symptoms
    AIDS, 102, 104
    immune deficiency, 101
    primary infections, 102
    unexplained, 139
Syndrome outlining AIDS, 17
Syphilis, 56, 91, 141
Syringes, transmitting AIDS, 39

T
T-cell growth factor
    see Interleukin II, 150
T-cells, 50, 106
T-lymphocyte(s), 44, 49, 101, 118, 134
    leukemia of, 26–27
T4-cells, 125, 138
T4-leukemia, 71
T4-Lymphocytes, 29–30, 33, 42–43,
    120–21, 123, 135, 137
T4-lymphophiliac HTLV, 49–50, 59
T4-trope virus, 60
T8-Lymphocytes, 120, 123
Taiwan, 53
Tanegashima, Island of, 54

INDEX

Target cells, 15
Tests for AIDS, 117, 121–22
Tetanus bacilli, 122
Thrombopenic purpura, 145
Thrush, 103
Thymus gland, 29
Tobago, Island of, 27, 56
Tomodensitometer, 104
Toxoplasma, 17, 21, 28, 44, 104–105, 115, 148
Tracer molecular probes, 14
Transfusion, 105
Transmission of AIDS, 32, 41, 81
  bisexual, 33
  through blood, 31–33, 37, 86
  chains of, 7, 35
  in Haiti, 41
  homosexual, 73, 78
  by injections, 39
  interhuman, 57
  through mucous membrane abrasions, 38
  through sexual contact, 33, 35, 37, 73, 78
  by syringes, 39
  woman-to-man, 36
Travenol, drug laboratory, 85
Treatments of AIDS, 146
Treponema pallidum, 91
Trinidad, 50
Tropical intestinal infections, 140
Tropical virus, 90
Tuberculosis, 115, 130
Tumors, malignant, 138

U
Undulant fever, 142
United States, black population in southwest, 55
University of Vienna, 18
Urine, 37, 126
Urticaria, 106, 110
Uruguay, 60
Uwajima, Island of, 51, 54

V
Vaccines, anti-hepatitis B, 88
Vaginal secretions, 37

Varicella-zona, 115
Vasco da Gama, 57
Vienna, University of, 18
Viral hypothesis of AIDS, 20
Virgin Islands, 50
Virus(es), 11
  African, 67
  AIDS, 13, 16, 42, 60, 81, 120
  AR-BO, 39
  carriers, 33, 50, 117–18, 151, 153
  cultivating in vitro, 71
  cytomegalic, 141–42
  Epstein-Barr, 47
  feline leukemia, 150
  FeLV, 45, 49
  hepatitis B, 34
  hepatotropic, 118
  herpes, 105
  HTLV, 54–55
  HTLV-I, 64
  HTLV-III/LAV, 84
  Human T-cell Leukemia, 70
  Human T-cell Lymphotropic, 70
  interhuman propogation, 42
  modifications in, 34
  presence in carrier, 49
  T4-trope, 60
  tropical, 90
  tropical AIDS, 92
Virus Amphitryons, 62

W
Warts, 22, 115
Weight loss, 107–108, 142
West Germany, 23
West Indies, 50
Women with AIDS, 35
World Health Organization, 80, 88

Y
Yamagushi (Honshu), Japan, 51, 54
Yeasts, 115
Yellow fever, 39

Z
Zaire, 21, 24, 26, 36, 38, 55, 65, 67, 80, 138, 153
Zonas, 110